Joy
Through
the
World

Joy Through

the World

An Allen D. Bragdon Book

Produced in cooperation with the U.S. Committee for UNICEF

Distributed by Dodd, Mead & Company New York

Designed and Published by
Allen D. Bragdon Publishers, Inc.
153 West 82nd Street
New York, N.Y. 10024
Produced in cooperation with
the U.S. Committee for UNICEF

Staff for this book:
Editor-in-Chief: Allen D. Bragdon
Research: Anne Pellowski
Editor: Karen Ringnalda Altman
Text: Wendy Murphy
Design and Layout: Stanley Moskowitz
Recipe Editing and Styling: Sidney Burstein
Assistant: Miriam Rubin
Recipes: United Nations Women's Guild,
Zaida Carleton, Jindra Hajsky, Hattie
Hoffman, Vlasta Kopal, Branca Rifai
Food Photography: Jesse Gerstein
Art Director, Food Photography: Stephanie
Schaffer
Craft Construction: Angela Erenberg
Craft Editing: Michael Eastman, Hannah
Selby
Craft Photography: Charles Biasiny-Rivera
Production Assistants: David Gamon, Hans
Schmitt

U.S. Committee for UNICEF:
Licensing Director: Richard Pordes
Photo Research: Melinda Greenblatt
Liaison: Gail Reiss
The publisher alone selected the geographical regions and customs represented in this book in order to illustrate colorful celebrations surrounding the winter solstice; therefore not every country or region of the world is included.
The textual designations used and the selection of pictorial material in these pages do not imply the expression of any opinion on the part of the Secretariat of the United Nations or of UNICEF.

The needlework designs and charts on page 116 are reprinted by permission of the designer, Lisbeth Perrone.

Distributed to the book trade by Dodd, Mead & Co.
79 Madison Avenue, New York, N.Y. 10016

Library of Congress Cataloging in
Publication Data

Main entry under title:
Joy through the world.
  Includes index.
  1. Christmas. 2. Winter—Folklore. 3. Holidays.
4. Holiday cookery. 5. Holiday decorations.
I. UNICEF. II. Allen D. Bragdon Publishers.
GT4985.J75 1985   394.2'683   85-14990
ISBN 0-916410-26-9

Printed in the U.S.A.

Photo Credits

Cover, front:UNICEF Card issued 1976. Cover, back:UNICEF card issued 1983. p. 2:UNICEF card forthcoming. p. 9:Leon V. Kofod, New York. p. 10, l:Leon V. Kofod, New York. p. 10, r:Air-India. p. 11, top:Air-India. p. 11, bot. l:UNICEF card issued 1958. p. 11, bot. r:Air-India. p. 15:Information Center on Children's Cultures, U.S. Committee for UNICEF. p. 19:Tourist Organization of Thailand, Bangkok. p. 20, l:Tourist Organization of Thailand, Bangkok. p. 20, r:Tourism Authority of Thailand, New York. p. 21, top:Tourist Organization of Thailand, Bangkok. p. 21, bot:Tourist Organization of Thailand, Bangkok. p. 24:Leon V. Kofod, New York. p. 25, top:UNICEF card issued 1979. p. 25, bot.:Tourism Authority of Thailand, New York. p. 31:From manuscript:Hanukha Piyyut. Mahzor. Hammelburg, Germany, 1348. Photo courtesy of Darmstadt Landesbibliothek (Ms. Orient, 13, fol. 33). p. 32, l:Hadassah, New York. p. 32, r:Leon V. Kofod, New York. p. 33, top:Aron/Art Resource, New York. p. 33, bot.:Jewish Museum/Art Resource, New York. p. 37, top:Consulate of Israel. p. 37, bot.:Consulate of Israel. p. 39, top:UNICEF card issued 1980. p. 41:Netherlands Board of Tourism, New York. p. 43, top:Leon V. Kofod, New York. p. 43, bot.:UNICEF card issued 1982. p. 47, top:Leon V. Kofod, New York. p. 47, bot.:3 F Produkties, Uithoorn, Netherlands. Courtesy of Netherlands Committee for UNICEF. p. 51:R. Rowan/Photo Researchers, New York. p. 52:Swedish Institute, Stockholm. p. 53, l:Photo by G. Algärd, Swedish Tourist Office, New York. p. 53, top r:Leon V. Kofod, New York. p. 53, bot. r:Skansen/Swedish Institute, Stockholm. p. 56:Swedish Tourist Board, New York. p. 57, top:Swedish Information Office, New York. p. 57, bot.:Swedish Information Service. p. 59, top:Swedish Information Service. p. 59, bot.:Swedish Information Service. p. 61:Swiss National Tourist Office. p. 62, l:Ricke/Austrian National Tourist Office, New York. p. 62, r:Leon V. Kofod, New York. p. 63, l:Swiss National Tourist Office. p. 63, top r:Uta Hoffman–German Information Service, New York. p. 63, bot. r:Uta Hoffman–German Information Service, New York. p. 66:R. Lans Christensen. p. 67, top:Swiss National Tourist Office. p. 67, bot.:R. Lans Christensen. p. 71:Polish Consulate, New York. p. 72:Polska Agencja Interpress. p. 73, top l:Polish Consulate, New York. p. 73, top r:Polish Consulate, New York. p. 73, bot. l:Polska Agencja Interpress. p. 73, bot. r:Polska Agencja Interpress. p. 77, top:Polish Consulate, New York. p. 77, bot.:Polish Consulate, New York. p. 83:Mathias Oppersdorff, New York. p. 84, l:Istituto Italiano di Cultura, New York. p. 84, r:Istituto Italiano di Cultura, New York. p. 85, l:Istituto Italiano di Cultura, New York. p. 85, r:Mathias Oppersdorff, New York. p. 89, l:Fotocolor E.N.I.T., Rome, Italy. Italian Government Travel Office, New York. p. 89, top r:Istituto Italiano di Cultura, New York. p. 89, bot. r:R. Lans Christensen. p. 93:Australian Tourist Commission. p. 94:Irish Tourist Board, New York. p. 95, top:Australian Tourist Commission. p. 95, bot.:Aódan O'Connor, Dublin. p. 96:UNICEF card issued 1979. p. 97, top l:Australian Information Service, New York. p. 97, top r:UNICEF card issued 1981. p. 97, bot. l:UNICEF card issued 1983. p. 101, top:Leon V. Kofod, New York. p. 101, bot.:British Tourist Authority. p. 105:Moldvay/Art Resource, New York. p. 106:Sapieha/Art Resource, New York. p. 107, top l:Leon V. Kofod, New York. p. 107, top r:Leon V. Kofod, New York. p. 107, bot.:Leon V. Kofod, New York. p. 108:UNICEF card issued 1978. p. 109, top:Museum of Cultural History, UCLA. p. 109, bot. l:Information Center on Children's Cultures, U.S. Committee for UNICEF. p. 109, bot. r:Collection of Joseph P. Egan, S.A., Hereford, Texas. p. 113, top l:UNICEF card issued 1979. p. 113, top r:UNICEF card issued 1983. p. 113, bot.:UNICEF card issued 1983. p. 117:UNICEF card issued 1983. p. 119:Canadian Consulate General, New York. p. 121, top:Leon V. Kofod, New York. p. 121, bot. l:Pierre St. Jacques, Canadian Consulate General, New York. p. 121, bot. r:Canadian Consulate General, New York. p. 122:Neil Portnoy, New York. p. 123, l:Leon V. Kofod, New York. p. 123, r:Leon V. Kofod, New York. p. 124, top:Leon V. Kofod, New York. p. 124, bot:UNICEF card issued 1980. p. 125, top:UNICEF card issued 1977. p. 125, bot.:Leon V. Kofod, New York. p. 129:Canadian Consulate General, New York. p. 133:Actualit, Agence Internationale de Presse, Brussels. p. 134, l:Joe Viesti. p. 134, r:Leon V. Kofod, New York. p. 135, l:Joe Viesti. p. 135, r:Actualit, Agence Internationale de Presse, Brussels. p. 143, top:UNICEF card issued 1974. p. 143, bot. l:UNICEF card issued 1983. p. 143, bot. r:Actualit, Agence Internationale de Presse, Brussels. p. 145:TASS from SOVFOTO. p. 146:UNICEF card issued 1976. p. 147:TASS from SOVFOTO. p. 151, top:TASS from SOVFOTO. p. 151, bot.:TASS from SOVFOTO. p. 155:Leon V. Kofod, New York. p. 156:Richard Gordon/Wheeler Pictures, New York. p. 157, l:Richard Gordon/Wheeler Pictures, New York. p. 157, top r:Leon V. Kofod, New York. p. 157, bot. r:Leon V. Kofod, New York. p. 158, l:Richard Gordon/Wheeler Pictures, New York. p. 158, r:Singapore Tourist Promotion Board, New York. p. 159, l:Richard Gordon/Wheeler Pictures, New York. p. 159, r:Leon V. Kofod, New York. p. 162:Japan Air Lines, New York. p. 163, top l:Richard Gordon/Wheeler Pictures, New York. p. 163, top r:Richard Gordon/Wheeler Pictures, New York. p. 163, bot.:Xinhua News Agency, New York. p. 165, top l:Leon V. Kofod, New York. p. 165, top r:Japan Air Lines, New York. p. 165, bot.:Japan Air Lines, New York.

Cover, *front:* Design for UNICEF card 1976 by Ivan Kirkov, Bulgaria Entitled "Christmas Night"; back: Design for UNICEF card 1983 by Alejandro Von-Waberer, Mexico, entitled "Making A Piñata."

Overleaf; Design for UNICEF card by Ljubomir Milinkov entitled "La Ronde du Monde."

INTRODUCTION

The U.S. Committee for UNICEF is proud to be cooperating in this holiday recipe and crafts book, *Joy Through the World*, published by Allen Bragdon. Our involvement in this book gives us the opportunity to help reach you, the reader, with an important message—that the needs of the world's children could be met, if only the necessary will, and some very modest means, were to be made available.

UNICEF—the United Nations Children's Fund—is working with governments in 115 developing countries to help bring about a virtual revolution in child survival techniques. By implementing four simple measures—mass immunization against childhood diseases, breast-feeding instead of bottle-feeding, oral rehydration for severely dehydrated children and growth monitoring—the lives of up to 20,000 children could be saved each day.

The U.S. Committee for UNICEF was formed to raise funds for UNICEF-assisted programs overseas and to increase American awareness of the needs of children. It is the largest volunteer-supported endeavour in the U.S. with over 3,000,000 adults and children participating. Each year, the President of the United States officially proclaims October 31st—Halloween—as National UNICEF Day and thousands of children "trick or treat" for UNICEF across the country. Through the sales of greeting cards, stationery, books and educational materials, the Committee raises additional funds.

The use of some of UNICEF's past greeting cards, to brighten the pages of this book, offers a rich and rewarding taste of UNICEF's world-famous greeting card program. Proceeds from the sales of this book, as with UNICEF cards, gifts and stationery, help provide vaccines, clean water, education and adequate nutrition for children in need.

The U.S. Committee for UNICEF would like to express its appreciation to the publishers for contributing a portion of their earnings from this book to help the world's children. We hope that the broad appeal of the book, and UNICEF's work, will help link the world through a commitment to children.

The U.S. Committee for UNICEF

CONTENTS

Introduction
the U.S. Committee for UNICEF

Diwali

Every Indian, rich or poor, looks forward to the joyous festival of Diwali, when every household comes alive with light. The word *Diwali* is a corruption of the Sanskrit word *Dipawali*, which literally translates as "row of lights." Festivities begin with the lighting of lamps on a moonless night in the month of Kartika (October-November). The celebration throughout the country continues for at least two or three days, but in some areas it may last as long as ten. By a happy coincidence, Diwali also marks the end of autumn and the beginning of the winter season in India.

The origins of Diwali are obscured in folklore and legend. Some say it commemorates the triumphal return of Rama and his bride, Sita, to his throne at Ayodhya after a fourteen-year exile, as told in the classic Indian epic, the *Ramayana*. Others believe it marks Krishna's destruction of Narakasura, the demon of filth, who stole the jewels of Aditi, mother of the gods, and who held 16,000 maidens captive. Still others trace its beginnings to the occasion on which Lakshmi, the goddess of wealth, was freed from prison in the Nether World. Another interpretation, unique to the people of the province of Bengal, is to honor the Pitris, departed souls who, they believe, return at this time each year.

In any case, every household marks the occasion by illuminating interiors, courtyards, outer walls, roofs, gates, and gardens with lights, as if to show the way for any or all of these mythic travelers. Traditionally, the lights were tiny oil lamps, called *diwa*, or more commonly *dipa*. Though many people continue to make dipa specifically for the occasion, candles, incandescent bulbs, and fluorescent lights are adding a modern touch to the occasion in many homes. To add color to brilliance, the merry-makers sometimes place glasses of colored water in front of the lights; the overall effect is like the twinkling of a million stars.

Celebration

The gala night of lights is typically preceded by several days of vigorous house cleaning. Families sweep their dwellings from top to bottom and, if they happen to live in a rural area, they apply a fresh coat of whitewash. Furniture gleams and bedding and cushions sport new covers. The women, who are in charge of decorating the household, hang garlands of brightly colored flowers and prepare stylized designs of birds and flowers, called *kolams* or *rangoli*, with colored rice flour, on doorsteps and in courtyards. People who can afford it treat themselves to new clothes for the occasion; those who cannot select whatever finery they already possess in preparation for the festivities.

The exhilarating notion of making a fresh start is at the heart of the Diwali celebration, and it carries over into the world of commerce, too. Merchants pay

Celebrating Diwali in Darjeeling. These special, large swings are put up in parks and schoolyards for the occasion.

up old debts at this time to insure that the goddess Lakshmi will bring them new wealth in the coming year, and presumably their customers are similarly inspired on this eve of the festival of lights. Merchants prepare and fill their stores' shelves with fresh merchandise. They decorate their shops lavishly and reward faithful employees with gifts of sweets and bonuses. Farmers, too, have reason to be especially thankful in that Diwali marks the beginning of a new growth cycle when winter wheat can be planted.

By custom, Indians commence the principal day of Diwali by taking a ceremonial bath with perfumed oils, followed by dressing in their best clothes. This being a time of special honor between siblings, a sister often prepares her brother's bath. She may also use saffron powder to paint an orange line on his head, and scatter a few grains of rice over him, as tokens of a long and happy life. In return a brother gives his sister gifts of new clothing or jewelry. When all members of the family are freshly dressed they join together in an elaborate and festive breakfast.

After the meal, the family goes out to savor the day, visiting friends, relatives, and colleagues with whom they exchange small gifts of sweets. The children, who sometimes receive a small amount of spending money for the occasion, buy firecrackers and toys at stalls also offering traditional painted clay and paper figurines. Almost every community has at least one street procession honoring Lakshmi as well as a Diwali fair. The day is not complete without the family's stopping to see the dancing bears, snake charmers, and trained monkeys who perform to the accompaniment of street musicians.

As the sun sets and night approaches, the whole family returns home to pray before the family altar, decorated with an image of Lakshmi. They tender offerings of flowers, sweets, and incense and light the lamps. Finally, everyone goes out into the streets to explode fireworks and to experience the beauty of the night, illuminated by the glow of a million lamps.

A crowd gathers to watch the swingers.

Diwali fireworks.

Public building illuminated for Diwali

Diwali festival of lights, a time of joy for every family.

Lighted dipa lamps.

Feasting

Breakfast being the only formal meal eaten on the day of Diwali, everything about it is special, from the new pots that may have been used in preparation, to the special flower-strewn tray called a *thali* on which dishes are served, to the number of different foods offered—as many as fourteen. *Chappaties*, a kind of flat bread eaten throughout the year, are sure to be served on this morning, too, but some uncommon dishes are also likely to appear.

No sooner is the breakfast meal over than everyone in new finery sets out to distribute special Diwali sweets. Indian sweets are of enormous variety; every region, even every city, has many specialties that are uniquely its own. But virtually all of these sweets can be categorized as either "dry" or semi-liquid and soft. Dry sweets include the confections known as *barfi*, and *laddus* are sweets typically made with milk, sugar, and porridge, though there are dozens of combinations that vary considerably from this best-known recipe. The softer sweets include *khir* and *halva*. K*hir* is a puddinglike dessert prepared with a base of rice, tapioca, lentils, sago, or pulped dates, to which are added cardamon and saffron. After cooking, the pudding is poured into cups to cool, then sprinkled with nuts. Halva is made from grated vegetables such as pumpkin, beets, carrots, or potatoes, which are boiled in milk, then fried in *ghee* or clarified butter along with sugar and flavorings. Still other sweets include *ras gulla*, cheese balls dipped in sugar syrup, *gulab jaman*, cheese balls fried in ghee and dipped in sugar syrup, and *jalebi*, which look somewhat like pretzels and are made of flour fried in ghee and coated with sugar.

Diwali sweets are often made at home, an indication of how special this day is considered to be, but since professional sweet-makers, called *halvais*, abound in India, there are plenty of opportunities to purchase these gifts outside the home if one so chooses. (In some streetside markets, it is customary to display the dry sweets in pyramids rising as high as 15 feet over the heads of strolling customers.)

The colorful sweets of Diwali are (clockwise, from lower right) jalebi, *pistachio halvah,* gulab jaman, *milk* barfi, *almond halvah, and carrot halvah.*

GULAB JAMAN

2 cups water
1½ cups granulated sugar
1 teaspoon rosewater (see Gajar Ka
　Halvah)
1 cup all-purpose flour
6 tablespoons non-fat dry milk powder
1 teaspoon baking powder
¼ cup milk
2 tablespoons ghee
Vegetable oil for frying

In a medium-sized heavy pot, mix water and sugar. Stir to dissolve. Bring to a boil over medium heat; wash down sides of pan with a brush dipped in cold water. Let syrup simmer 15 to 20 minutes or until slightly thickened. Stir in rosewater to flavor and set aside. Meanwhile, in medium bowl mix flour, milk powder, and baking powder. Add milk and ghee. Knead to a smooth dough. Divide and roll into about twelve 1-inch balls. Heat oil to 350°F. (180°C) in a heavy, deep skillet over medium heat. Add balls, a few at a time, and fry until golden brown, 3 to 5 minutes, turning once. Remove oil and let drain briefly on paper towels. Plunge into syrup. Repeat with rest of balls. Let sit in syrup 1 to 2 hours; remove before serving. Makes 25 Gulab Jaman.

BADAM PISTAZ BARFI

1 tablespoon plus 1 teaspoon ghee
　(clarified butter)
4 cups milk
1 cup granulated sugar
1 cup blanched almonds, ground
1 cup skinned natural pistachios, ground
2 teaspoons rose water (see Gajar Ka
　Halvah)
1 teaspoon ground cardamom

Grease an 8-inch round cake pan with 1 teaspoon ghee. In a large heavy saucepan, bring milk to a boil over high heat. Reduce heat to low and cook about ½ hour or until reduced to consistency of heavy cream, stirring frequently. Add sugar and cook, stirring, 10 minutes more. Stir in almonds and pistachios and cook 10 minutes more, stirring constantly. Stir in remaining tablespoon ghee and, stirring constantly, cook 5 to 10 minutes or until mixture leaves sides of pan. Remove from heat; stir in rosewater and cardamom. Scrape into cake pan and smooth with spatula. Let cool about 30 minutes. Cut into diamonds. Makes 25 diamonds.

GHEE

Melt 2 pounds unsalted butter in a medium-sized heavy pot over low heat. Let simmer 15 to 20 minutes. (This causes the water to evaporate.) Remove from heat when the milky white residue turns to golden particles. Strain through a double thickness cheesecloth into bowl. Let cool and store in refrigerator. Yields about 2 cups of ghee (clarified butter).

ALMOND HALVAH

½ pound whole unblanched almonds
2 cups granulated sugar
1 cup ghee

5 cardamom seeds, ground
Pinch of saffron dissolved in 1 teaspoon
　warm milk.

Soak almonds overnight in water to cover. Drain, rub off skins, and grind to a fine paste in food processor, blender, or nut grinder. Put sugar in a medium-sized heavy pot. Stir in enough water to dissolve sugar and make a thin syrup. Stir in almonds. Over low heat, gradually stir in ghee. Cook, stirring, until mixture leaves sides of pan. Stir in saffron and ground cardamom. Lightly grease an 8-inch round cake pan with ghee. Pour in almond mixture. Cool until set. Cut into desired shapes.

CARROT HALVAH
GAJAR KA HALVAH

6 cups milk
1 pound carrots, grated
1 cup ghee
2 cups granulated sugar
¼ pound blanched slivered almonds
8 cardamom seeds
2 cups heavy cream
2 teaspoons rosewater (*kewra*)
4 pieces edible silver leaf (*waraq*)
　—optional
2 tablespoons pistachio nuts, skinned
　and chopped

In a medium-sized heavy pot, bring milk to a boil over low heat. Stir in carrots; simmer slowly, stirring occasionally until all milk is absorbed. Add ghee, stirring constantly; add sugar, almonds, and cardamom seeds. Cook 5 minutes, stirring constantly. Stir in cream and rosewater. Stirring constantly, cook until the butter begins to separate slightly. Remove from heat. Spread halvah evenly in large baking pan; cover with edible silver leaf, if desired. Sprinkle with pistachio nuts. Let cool; then cut into small squares. Rosewater is available in Middle Eastern specialty stores and in pharmacies.

Detail of the goddess Lakshmi from a Diwali street poster. New Delhi, India.

Giving

The tiny earthenware *dipa* lamps, with which Indians light their households during the Festival of Lights, are often very simply made of dried, baked earthenware. Basically, each is formed from tiny balls of clay, with a bowl hollowed out in the center to hold oil and a lip formed on one edge to hold the dry end of the wick. Lamps by the dozens may then be lined up along window ledges, roof tops, and walkways, where they can be enjoyed by those outside as well as those at home.

Diwali toys, small, rudely-painted clay or papier-mâché toys that are traditional at this season, are also handmade, either at home or by artisans in the market-place. The clay is the same as that used in dipa lamps, and after the clay toys are fired in the oven they are painted with simple tempera colors.

LAMP

Materials: self-hardening clay; pencil; wicks (obtainable where candle-making supplies are sold); vegetable or corn oil.

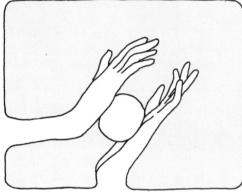

1. Roll portion of clay into 2½" (6.25cm) ball between palms of hands. Then put on flat surface and press to form disc 1¼" (3cm) high.

2. While turning disc, work edges with fingers and press thumbs into center to achieve flat-bowl shape.

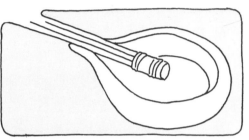

3. To form lip, pull clay out and press against pencil.

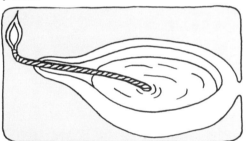

4. Allow clay to dry. Then coil wick and put in bowl with end extending ½" (1.25cm) past lip. Pour in just enough oil to cover wick coil.

PAPIER-MACHE TURTLE

Materials: newspapers; ¾" (2cm) masking tape; 4" (10cm) round cardboard coaster or disc; small bowl; pie tin; ½ cup (70gm) flour; water; white household glue; piece of thin cardboard; ruler; 5" (12.7cm) pointed pencil stub; acrylic or poster paints; brushes.

1. Cut newspaper pages in half along fold and tear lengthwise into ½" x 11" (1.3 x 28cm) strips.

2. In bowl, slowly stir ¼ cup water (65ml) into ½ cup (70gm) flour until smooth. Now stir in enough water plus 1 T. (15ml) white glue to make thin paste. Pour paste into wide, shallow bowl or pie tin.

TAPE CRUMPLED NEWSPAPER TO BASE   COASTER

3. Crumple two 14" x 22" (35 x 56cm) pages or equivalent of newspaper and securely tape to coaster or disc to form a turtleshell mold.

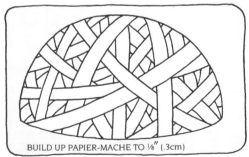

BUILD UP PAPIER-MACHE TO ⅛" (.3cm)

4. Pull a strip of paper through paste and apply from bottom to top of mold, around and back to bottom. Repeat starting in different places and criss-crossing strips until glue and paper reach depth of at least ⅛" (.3cm) over entire surface. Set aside for several hours to dry, in sunlight or near heat if possible.

16

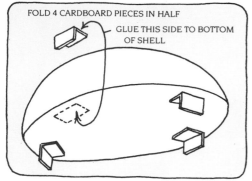

FOLD 4 CARDBOARD PIECES IN HALF

GLUE THIS SIDE TO BOTTOM OF SHELL

5. Meanwhile, to make legs cut 4 thin cardboard pieces ¾" x 1½" (2 x 4cm). Fold each to ¾" (2cm) square and glue upper square of each piece close to edge of shell's underside where you wish to position legs. Angle legs away from body slightly. Fill out legs by wrapping with strips of paper and glue while continuing to build up shell thickness to ¼" (.65cm).

What child, or adult for that matter, would not treasure this tortoise of papier-mâché?

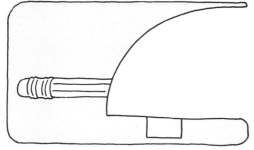

6. For head, poke pointed end of 5" (12.7cm) pencil stub through papier-mâché between front legs and just above coaster. Then drive pencil through until it touches back of shell.

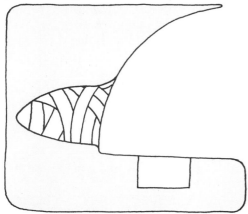

7. Apply paper strips and glue around pencil to achieve gently pointed shape of turtle head. Set aside to dry thoroughly, then sand off rough edges. Turtle is now ready for painting or appliquéing.

Thousands of clay Diwali lamps, fueled with ghee (clarified butter) and a simple string wick, glow in Indian homes during the Diwali "Festival of Lights."

17

Loy Krathong

On a full-moon night in the twelfth lunar month, usually mid-November, the Thai people gather at the waters' edge to celebrate the festival of Loy Krathong, or Floating Lotus Cups. Rivers, canals, ponds, and pools are transformed into twinkling gardens of light as families and friends gather after dark to set afloat lovely lotus-shaped paper boats, all containing candles.

Several explanations exist for the origins of this festival of lights. One traces it to the time of King Ramakhamhaeng of Sukhothai who reigned over the Thai-Khmer some seven hundred years ago. As the story goes, one of the king's wives, Nang Nophames, was accompanying the king as he made his annual pilgrimage by boat from riverside temple to temple. So devoted was she that as she rode she sought some means to please both her husband and Lord Buddha, and the notion came to her of placing an offering upon the water where it could be seen by all. Losing no time turning her idea into action, she prepared a fragile paper lantern in the form of a lotus flower, which to the Thais symbolizes the flowering of the human spirit. This lantern she then filled with carved birds and a candle, and set it afloat. Sure enough, the king saw the queen's invention and was so delighted that he decreed that henceforth all his subjects should follow this custom on this one night of the year.

Another Thai legend traces Loy Krathong to the still more ancient practice of propitiating the Mother of Water, Mae Khongkha. The lotus cups, which often contain small coins, are humble tokens of apology for the impurities which people, through their thoughtless ways, have permitted to seep into her life-giving waters during the year. Out of this belief has sprung the idea of the festival as a time of renewal; the Thais cast their sins upon the water and begin anew. Young lovers often take advantage of this joyous occasion to declare their mutual devotion.

Still another possible source of the festival relates to legends surrounding Gautama Buddha, the Indian philosopher who founded the religion of Buddhism to which most Thais adhere. According to at least one of these stories, the festival honors the lotus blossoms that sprang up when Buddha took his first baby steps; or another, the footprint he left on the shores of the Nammada River when he departed the earthly life.

Whatever the origin of Loy Krathong, this evening holiday is celebrated throughout Thailand by both adults and children with great good humor and delight.

A Thai woman places her krathong in the water.

Celebration

Nearly every Thai floats his or her own krathong as part of the festival observance. The designs they use today seem nearly infinite in ingenuity and variety, though of course some still retain the traditional lotus leaf shape. But the modern observance of the festival is enhanced by the element of cheerful competition involved in creating the krathongs and adds to the fun of the affair. Consequently, though vendors can be counted on to sell ready-made krathongs to anyone who comes to the waterside unprepared, most people prefer to make their own. Children, especially, are encouraged to try their hand at it with, if necessary, an assist from parents.

Thais may spend the day going about their normal pursuits—jobs or school—but many choose this occasion to make a pilgrimage to one of the major temples. Because fairs coincide with every holiday, this kind of excursion is sure to be as much fun as it is meritorious. At the center of the fair is almost certainly a company of actors putting on one of the traditional Thai tales of demonic derring-do. And all around, groups of dancers perform, snake charmers fascinate, bands play, and temporary stalls offer everything from tasty foods to toys and silk goods.

As night falls, families everywhere return home to share a festive dinner. Then all proceed to the nearest body of water—for many this journey is merely a matter of a few feet, since living on a canal or river is common in this watery land. After singing one of the traditional songs associated with the day, each participant lights a candle, and perhaps a piece of incense too, and launches a floating token, saying a prayer at the same time. Barges of banana leaves, boats of paper, lotus blossoms, decorated coconut shells, folded bits of colored paper, elaborate constructs in the shape of temples, forts, and palaces, all slide gently into the current and begin their journey. Each Thai is hoping that his or her krathong will stay afloat and its candle remain lighted until the little vessel is out of sight, for this is a sign that the person's prayer will be answered.

The evening ends with fireworks, the glow of the krathongs gradually flickering out as the skies become bright with beautiful cascades of colored lights.

A family watches its krathong, hoping the lights will not go out.

Tiny krathongs on the water.

Thais gather to set their krathongs afloat.

The glow from candles and fireworks lights
up rivers and canals.

Our festival meal includes a pineapple half, scooped out to contain a fresh pineapple and apple chutney flavored with ginger and garlic. The barbecued chicken (lower right) is subtly flavored with 1 tablespoon fish sauce, a common ingredient in Thai cuisine. The dessert (upper right), the Golden Silk, is a thread of egg yolk gently poached and served in a sugar syrup.

PINEAPPLE-APPLE CHUTNEY

1½ cups granulated sugar
½ cup distilled white vinegar
2 tablespoons minced crystalized ginger
2 teaspoons minced garlic
1½ teaspoons salt
1 teaspoon chili powder
½ teaspoon each ground cinnamon and ginger
2 cups diced fresh pineapple
2 apples, peeled, cored and diced
½ cup dark raisins

In deep enamel pot or Dutch oven mix together first 7 ingredients. Bring to a boil over moderate heat. Add remaining ingredients. Heat to a simmer and cook about 1 hour, lightly covered, stirring occasionally until fruit is soft and sauce has thickened. Fruit should still retain its shape. Cool and refrigerate. Serve in pineapple shell if desired.

THAI BARBECUED CHICKEN

1 tablespoon Nuc Man (Thai fish sauce available in Oriental markets)
2 medium cloves garlic
½ teaspoon each turmeric, paprika, and freshly ground black pepper
4 whole chicken legs
2 tablespoons vegetable oil

Heat barbecue or broiler. In blender or food processor or with mortar and pestle, make a paste of fish sauce, garlic, and spices. Make 4 diagonal slits on each chicken leg. Rub paste into cuts and over surface of chicken. Brush with oil. Barbecue or broil about 35 minutes, turning several times. Makes 4 servings.

COCONUT MILK

1 whole fresh coconut
6 cups hot water

Carefully crack coconut; drain and discard white liquid. Extract meat from shell and peel brown skin with vegetable peeler. Grate or coarsely purée coconut meat using a food processor. In medium bowl, combine grated coconut and 2 cups hot water. Let stand 5 minutes. Line a second bowl with cheesecloth; pour in coconut mixture. Squeeze and twist cheesecloth to extract liquid. Set aside strained liquid. Repeat entire process using another 2 cups hot water. Repeat twice using 1 cup water each time. Discard grated coconut. Makes about 6 cups coconut milk.

SIAMESE CHICKEN CURRY

Vegetable oil
A 2½-pound chicken, cut in 8 pieces
1 tablespoon curry powder
1 teaspoon salt
1 teaspoon sugar
1 teaspoon ground coriander
½ teaspoon red pepper flakes
4 medium potatoes, peeled
6 cups Coconut Milk (see Recipe)

In Dutch oven, heat about ¼-inch vegetable oil. Fry chicken pieces until golden on both sides. Add spices and toss chicken until evenly coated. Add potatoes and coconut milk. Simmer uncovered, stirring occasionally, until liquid is reduced to about 4 cups, and chicken is cooked through, about 1 hour. Serve with rice. Makes about 4 servings.

THE GOLDEN SILK

12 egg yolks
2 cups sugar
2 cups water

Use a small tin can with top removed and a hole the size of a pencil point punched in middle of the bottom. Remove white membrane that holds yolks in place. Gently simmer water and sugar about 15 minutes until it becomes syrup. Beat egg yolks only enough to give mixture a uniform shade. Place tin can over boiling syrup or use a funnel with a very fine tip. Place 1 tablespoon of egg yolk in can, allowing yolk to stream into boiling syrup; it becomes a golden thread. Rotate can to form rosette. Remove from syrup. Place in stemmed glass. Repeat for each serving. Serve with syrup. Makes 6 servings.

Thais course over the water as part of a national festival celebrating their ancient heritage as a free people. (The word Thai means "free.")

Anonymous batik (detail).

Thai traditional costumes.

25

Giving

The krathong, which means lotus blossom, is traditionally made at home by parents and children in the days just preceding the festival. Most often the pretty device is fashioned from a banana leaf, folded so that it can float upon the water for several hours. Sometimes, however, it is made from tissue paper or even foil.

They cut the leaves into large circles and scallop or otherwise embellish their turned-up edges to imitate a lotus blossom. They then fill the centers with a piece of incense, a slim candle, and perhaps some flowers.

Gift giving is not a significant feature of the day, but vendors selling inexpensive little woven toys, fashioned from strips of palm leaves, are likely to be out in force on such an evening, and children inevitably persuade their parents to buy them one or more of these little creatures.

Both the krathong and the woven toy are easy to make, even without access to Thai materials, as shown below. Metal foil and manila paper products are substitutes that are readily available almost anywhere in the world.

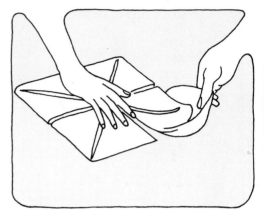

5. Turn square back over and carefully unfold 8 petals, 1 at a time, until form looks like an open blossom.

KRATHONG

1. Reinforce the edges of the foil on the dull side with transparent plastic tape.

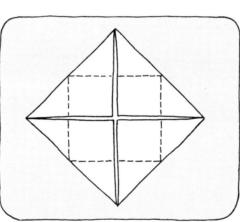

3. Fold corners down to center. Be careful not to overlap edges. Fold newly formed corners down to center a second time. Now fold corners down to center a third time.

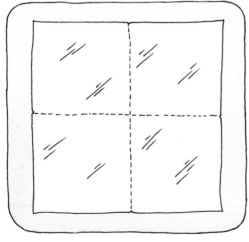

2. With the shiny side up, fold foil square in half vertically and unfold. Fold in half horizontally and unfold.

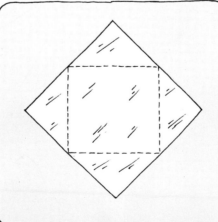

4. Turn over square and again fold corners to center, then unfold.

6. Light candle and drip melted wax in bottom of cup. Press candle into wax.

26

Families prepare for the festival by folding banana leaves, tissue paper, or foil into krathongs, which means "lotus blossom." The folds are so clever that these tiny boats will stay afloat for hours after they are set out on the moving rivers and quiet lakes where their cargo of flowers and a tiny candle twinkles in the night.

Sometimes the leaves or foil is folded into the shape of an open box and laden with fruit as an offering to the river or lake. It is set afloat on the night of the full moon when Loy Krathong is celebrated in the twelfth lunar month.

WOVEN FISH

People in Thailand weave the stiff, dried leaves of palm trees into shapes similar to the way *origami* paper-folding is practiced in the Far East.

Pla Tak Pien

Materials: 2 strips of palm leaf or thick paper, about 14″ x ½″; 2 short strips, about 2″ long. A legal size manila folder is 14″ long.

For clarity in the diagram strip A is shown as white, and strip B shaded.

1. Mark ends of strip A, 1 and 2; of B, 3 and 4.

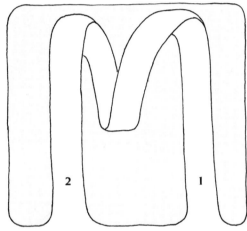

2. With strip A form two small loops.

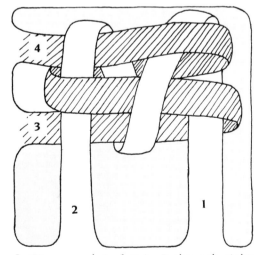

3. Weave end 4 of strip B through right loop; over and around left loop; through right loop again; bend in front of right loop and through left loop.
4. Bend end 3 of strip B behind right loop and through left loop.
5. Pull all four ends to tighten.

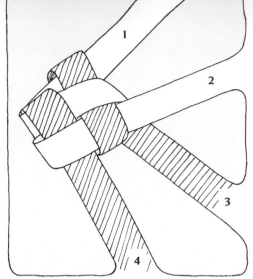

6. Reverse so that woven corner faces left.
7. Bend 4 upwards, under 3, and bend 1 downwards over 2 and 4.

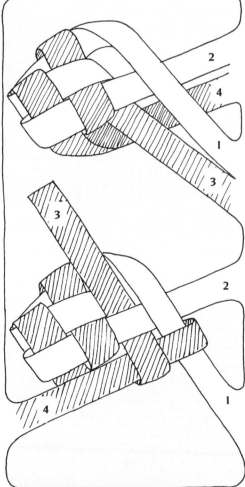

8. Bend 4 down over 1 and 3, and bend 3 upward, weaving under 2.
9. Tighten, but not too tight.

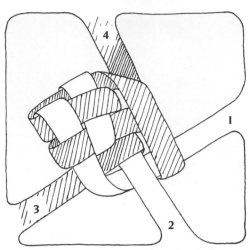

10. Reverse fish, uncompleted side facing you.

11. Weave as follows: bend 1 downward; weave 2 upward over 1, and under next strip.

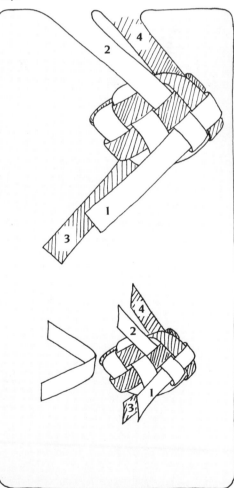

12. Tighten cut ends to form fins. Fold short strip to make tail. Attach with tape.

28

Hanukkah

Jewish people celebrate Hanukkah, which means "deliverance," around the time of the winter solstice, when the year's decline into darkness ends and the days begin to lengthen again. It is a joyous eight-day-long period, marking the climax of three years of Jewish resistance against the Syrian Greeks, some twenty-one centuries ago. Led by Judas Maccabaeus, a small band of freedom fighters retaliated against their Gentile overlords, who were systematically suppressing all expressions of Jewish faith.

After scoring a series of guerilla victories against the more numerous, better armed, regular armies of King Antiochus, the Maccabees recaptured Jerusalem and set out to reclaim the Holy Temple which had been profaned by pagan worship. On the twenty-fifth day of the month of Kislev in 165 B.C.E., the Jews began their rituals of rededication. Following Jewish law, the priests set out to rekindle the Great Menorah, or candelabrum, in which burned the Eternal Flame. But the priests, searching for consecrated oil, were consternated to find only enough for one night's burning. To prepare additional lamp oil would take days, they knew, and they went ahead with their ceremonies with heavy hearts, fearing they would be unable to continue in the days ahead. But to their increasing astonishment, the lamps continued to burn for eight days. The Jews saw this as a clear sign from God that their faith was enduring, and they have celebrated the two-thousand-year-old miracle of deliverance ever since.

High priest kindling the temple menorah, from a fourteenth-century manuscript.

Celebration

Modern-day Jews celebrate the Miracle at the Temple, the transformation of spiritual darkness into light, with the ritual lighting of candles in every home. For this purpose they use a special Hanukkah menorah, which has nine lamps or candle branches rather than the usual seven. The ninth light, typically located in the center of the menorah and raised slightly above the others, is designated the *shammash*, or server light, its sole purpose being to provide the flame for kindling the other holy lights. Every evening during the eight days of Hanukkah the family gathers around the menorah. One of the parents lights the shammash, after which the family recites three traditional blessings. On the first night, the wielder of the shammash lights the taper farthest to the right; then all family members join in song. And on each succeeding night, they add another light to the first, symbolizing the new day.

When the religious observance is over, the family joins in games and other pleasant amusements. Families with young children present their youngsters with a modest gift on each of the nights. Historians believe that this tradition began centuries ago when Jewish parents gave their offspring small amounts of money to reward them for learning their Torah well and gave their teachers money for doing their job well, too. Nowadays the gifts may range from money to Jewish books and ceremonial art to all manner of secular toys.

Israel has added a new tradition to the public observance of Hanukkah—a torchlight race. Run between Modin and Jerusalem, it reminds Jews of the town where the Maccabees first rose up against their Greek oppressors and the Holy City where they won their final victory and the first observance of Hanukkah began.

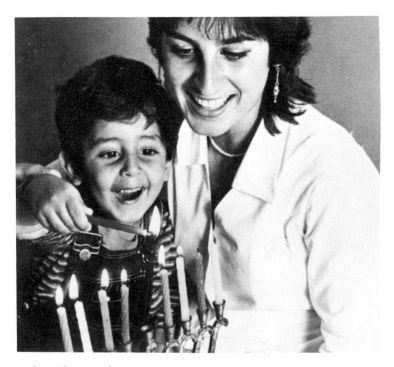

Lighting the menorah.

Holiday parade in an Israeli community.

Israeli child spinning a dreydl.

Eighteenth-century Polish dreydls.

Feasting

The traditional foods often served on the first night of Hanukkah recall the legends surrounding the celebration. The most beloved of these foods are *latkes*, or pancakes. According to some historians these fried treats are eaten in remembrance of the miraculous oil that burned for eight days in the rededicated Holy Temple. Others believe that latkes were an early kind of "fast food," whipped up behind the battle lines by the Maccabean women during the resistance.

Nowadays, latkes are commonly made with a batter whose basic ingredient is potatoes, a staple of the diet of Eastern European Jews. But Sephardic Jews, whose diet more closely resembles that of their ancient forbears in this particular, make their Hanukkah latkes with pot cheese. The cheese recalls symbolically the heroic tale of Judith, who, like the Maccabees, is said to have delivered the children of Israel from their enemies; this time, though, the enemy was the Assyrian Holofernes and the place was Bethulia, a city brought to desperation by a forty-day siege.

According to legend, Judith, a beautiful and seductive widow of the tribe of Simeon, won her way into the camp of Holofernes, disarming him with her wit and charm. Thoroughly smitten, the general invited her to his tent, whereupon she offered him as tribute a quantity of fine cheese. The Assyrian, who evidently was a man of great appetites, ate himself into a fierce thirst—to which Judith responded by offering him a perhaps excessive quantity of delicious wine. In due course, the well-fed and watered Holofernes fell into a deep sleep, and the courageous Judith, seizing his sword, beheaded the tyrant and slipped away to spread the good news. Holofernes's followers, upon discovering their leader's unfortunate demise, fled in disarray, and the Israelites, saved from destruction once again, fell to rejoicing.

In Israel, where latkes are a staple of most families' diet throughout the year, they are often dressed up for the holiday season with garnishes of fruit, applesauce, apricot puree, or other sweet toppings.

No night of the Hanukkah season is marked for feasting in a way comparable to the Christian Christmas, but the first night is somewhat more special than the others, especially among American Jews. A special roast bird may indeed be the climax of this inaugural celebration.

A large platter overflowing with latkes—crisp potato, on the left, and golden cheese dusted lightly with powdered sugar. To complement the flavors, serve applesauce or garnish with a dollop of sour cream and chopped scallions. The menorah is lighted and the chocolate gelt rewards the winner of the next spin of the dreydl.

HOT MINTED TEA
Fresh mint leaves, chopped
Tea leaves or bags

Add chopped mint leaves to tea pot along with tea leaves or bags. Add boiling water and let steep 5 minutes. Pour into cups.

SOUR CREAM TOPPING FOR LATKES
1 cup sour cream
1 tablespoon sliced scallions
½ teaspoon salt
½ teaspoon ground cumin
¼ teaspoon freshly ground black pepper

In small bowl, stir together all ingredients until blended. Chill and serve as an accompaniment to Potato or Cheese Latkes.

APPLESAUCE
4 cups cored, quartered apples
¼ cup water
1 tablespoon honey
1 teaspoon freshly squeezed lemon juice
½ teaspoon ground cinnamon

In large heavy pot, bring apples and water to a boil. Lower heat, cover, and simmer 10 to 15 minutes, stirring frequently until apples are soft. Purée in batches in blender or food processor until quite smooth. Push mixture through a sieve into a medium bowl. Stir in remaining ingredients. Serve warm or chilled as an accompaniment to Potato or Cheese Latkes.

CARDAMOM COFFEE
Whole cardamom seeds
Coffee beans

Add 1 cardamom seed to beans for each 1-cup measure coffee when grinding beans. Or add 1 cardamom seed to each 1-cup measure ground coffee. Brew as for coffee.

POTATO LATKES
5 medium potatoes
1 medium onion, chopped
2 large eggs, lightly beaten
3 tablespoons flour or matzo meal

Salt and pepper to taste
½ cup vegetable oil
Applesauce or sour cream and chopped
   scallions

Scrub and peel potatoes. Finely grate into large bowl. Stir in onion, eggs, flour, salt, and pepper until smooth. In large skillet heat 2 to 3 tablespoons of the oil over medium heat. Drop large spoonfuls of batter into oil and fry about 4 minutes, turning once, until golden and crisp. Drain on paper towels. Continue with remaining batter, adding more oil as necessary. Serve with applesauce and/or sour cream.

CHEESE LATKES
2 cups small curd cottage cheese
3 eggs, lightly beaten
1 cup all-purpose flour
1 tablespoon granulated sugar
1 teaspoon baking powder
½ teaspoon salt
Vegetable oil
Confectioners' sugar

In medium bowl, stir all ingredients until smooth. In large skillet, heat about ¼-inch oil over medium heat. Drop about ¼ cup batter into oil and fry about 4 minutes, turning once, unti golden. Repeat with remaining batter. Sift confectioners' sugar, if desired.

Israeli family lighting the menorah.

Ancient menorahs.

Giving

The practice of giving to children on Hanukkah may derive from the tradition of handing out small bonuses, known as Hanukkah *gelt* (gold), to children who had been diligent in studying the Torah in the preceding months. Hanukkah gelt continues to be a traditional gift, though now it may be only one of several modest surprises bestowed during the eight-night-long festivities. Many parents still take the term gelt literally and give small amounts of money with which the children then buy themselves treats, but another kind of gelt prevalent on this holiday is coin-shaped candy wrapped in gold foil.

Another traditional gift of Hanukkah is the handmade *dreydl*, a four-sided spinning top. In times past, a family made these cheerful toys at home of clay or lead, often using molds that had been passed down from one generation to another. Some families still preserve the tradition of making Hanukkah dreydls but others purchase their tops. Dreydls are now available in a variety of materials, including wood and even plastic.

Every dreydl is inscribed with the Hebrew characters for *nun, gimel, hay,* and *shin* on its four sides. The letters are said to stand for Nes *gadol haya sham*, meaning "a great miracle happened there" (at the Holy Temple), but to generations of Jewish children the characters have also come to mean *nikhts* (Yiddish for nothing), *gantz* (everything), *halb* (half), and *shtell-arein* (put in), and the spinning top the essential element in playing a jolly game of chance. As gambling of any sort is forbidden under rabbinical law throughout most of the year, considerable excitement attends the game and adults frequently find themselves joining the fun with an enthusiasm equal to their children's.

To play, participants put an equal number of tokens—nuts, pennies, Hanukkah gelt, or the like—in the kitty. Each player, in turn, spins the dreydl and, depending upon which of the four Hebrew characters faces up when the toy topples, the player wins nothing from the pot, half the pot, all of it, or must add to it (usually two tokens) from his or her reserve. As the simple game progresses, players are forced to drop out when their reserves are depleted. The winner is the survivor who ends up with everyone else's tokens.

DREYDL

Materials: 2 pieces of cardboard, 2" x 4" (5 x 10cm) and 3" x 3" (7.5 x 7.5cm); ruler; pencil; acrylic or poster paints; brushes; masking tape; household glue.

1. Starting from 2" (5cm) edge of 2" x 4" (5 x 10cm) cardboard, make 3 folds 1" (2.5cm) apart. Then fold in half lengthwise. You now have eight 1" (2.5cm) squares in 2 rows.

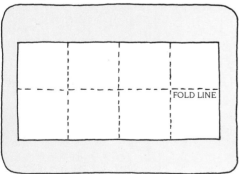

FOLD LINE

2. With ruler and pencil, mark bottom edge at ½", 1½", 2½", and 3½" (1.25, 3.8, 6.3, and 8.9cm). Draw lines between these points and 2 upper corners of each lower square. Cut along these lines with scissors.

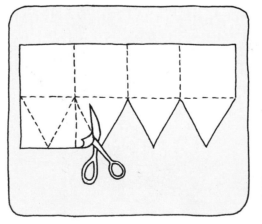

3. Fold together along lines to form box with open top and pointed bottom. Tape seams.

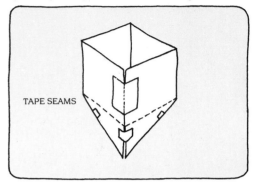

TAPE SEAMS

4. From 3" x 3" (7.5 x 7.5cm) cardboard, cut away 1" (2.5cm) square at all 4 corners leaving cross shape. Fold down arms, glue them to sides of box and let dry. Now box has top.

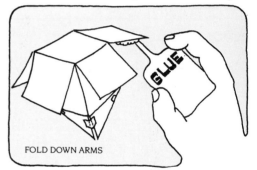

GLUE

FOLD DOWN ARMS

5. Draw diagonal lines between opposite corners of top surface to mark center and push sharply pointed pencil through top and bottom.

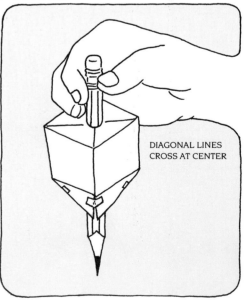

DIAGONAL LINES
CROSS AT CENTER

6. Paint dreydl and, when dry, paint the Hebrew letters, one letter on each side, in the order shown below. Blue on white or vice-versa (the colors of Israel) would be appropriate.

ש	ה	ג	נ
SHIN	HAY	GIMEL	NUN

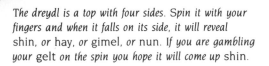

The dreydl is a top with four sides. Spin it with your fingers and when it falls on its side, it will reveal shin, or hay, or gimel, or nun. If you are gambling your gelt on the spin you hope it will come up shin.

Sinterklaas

In the Netherlands, the Dutch eagerly await the evening of December 5th each year, for it is Sinterklaas Avond or St. Nicholas Eve. The date marks the birthday some seventeen centuries ago of Nicholas, the "boy bishop of Myra" (a city in Asia Minor), whose deeds of generosity and kindness are legendary. In one particularly celebrated instance, for example, he dropped gifts of gold down the chimney of an impoverished family whose daughters, lacking the necessary dowry to marry, were about to sell themselves into slavery. The money that saved them from this desperate fate turned up miraculously in stockings they had hung by the fire to dry.

The Dutch, putting their own particular twist on the tale, have made the birthday into an occasion of national merrymaking for young and old alike. They turn out en masse to greet St. Nicholas, who arrives by ship in Amsterdam, the capital, three weeks before the special evening that bears his name. Dressed in his bishop's attire—white robes, a scarlet cape, miter, and carrying his crozier—St. Nicholas appears seated on a handsome white horse. He proceeds down the gangplank, at the foot of which he is greeted by the Lord Mayor. Dignitaries, a brass band, floats, and a horde of cheering youngsters then fall into line behind the long-awaited visitor, and the whole colorful parade heads toward the city's main square to be received by the Royal Family.

Sinterklaas is always accompanied by *Zwarte Piet*, or Black Pete, who is part Devil incarnate, part prankster. Pete dresses in the flamboyantly embroidered tunic, puffed velvet breeches, and plumed cap of sixteenth-century Spanish courtiers—the two visitors are supposed to winter somewhere in Spain—and carries several props of his trade. The first is a big red ledger in which is recorded the year's behavior report on every Dutch child; the second is a handful of birch rods useful in bringing unruly children into line; and the third is a big sack of goodies—fruits, candies, and cookies, especially those nugget-shaped, spice-filled delights called *pepernoten*—for rewarding youngsters who have gained Sinterklaas's favor. The bag is also supposed to be large enough to hold a naughty child or two, in the unlikely event that the bishop decides to take someone back to Spain for a year's discipline.

In Amsterdam, St. Nicholas's arrival signals the beginning of the holiday season. In succeeding days smaller towns and cities reenact similar ceremonies with Sinterklaas appearing variously aboard barge, motorcycle, wagon, bicycle, helicopter, or whatever mode of locomotion is at hand, and greeters arriving in throngs to appreciate the moment and join in the pageantry.

In virtually every household in the Netherlands people are abustle with preparations for one or more personal visits from the bishop and Black Pete, who are believed to spend their nights scurrying across rooftops, eavesdropping down chimneys, and even making occasional descents to hearths below. Just in case the pair might be in the neighborhood, children fill their shoes with carrots and straw, snacks for the bishop's horse, before they go to bed. They hold steadfastly

Sinterklaas and Zwarte Piet.

to the hope that Pete—who does the actual scampering—will stop at their hearth, find the offerings, and pass them on to the bishop, who will be so impressed with their thoughtfulness that he will return the favor with some gift of his own. Some families also resort to singing special songs and drawing pictures—hoping that the sounds and sights will draw Sinterklaas and Pete near. These blandishments appear to work, for over the next few days the pair usually visits several times, as evidenced by the little candies found some mornings in the children's shoes. The excitement grows, not surprisingly, as the evening of December 5th draws closer.

December 6th is celebrated with more family doings, after which everyone settles down to prepare for First Christmas Day, on December 25th, Second Christmas on the 26th, New Year's, and Three Kings Day on January 6th. Each of these occasions has its special traditions, some observed with a certain religious formality, and some marked with rituals that are traceable back to pagan times, but none holds the special affection of the Dutch as much as Sinterklaas Avond.

Celebration

Most Dutch households observe Sinterklaas Avond with an informal evening gathering of favorite relatives and friends. Sometimes St. Nick and Pete drop by in person just one last time—to deliver mock lectures on each guest's doings during the preceding year and to suggest possible areas of improvement. More often, however, they make themselves known by a mysterious knock heard at the door or window after the last guest has arrived. When everyone turns to see where the noise is coming from, a black hand reaches through the opening to toss a great quantity of sweets into the crowd, and disappears in an instant. The stage is now set for an evening of fun and good food.

Following a festive dinner is the ritual of gift giving, and the Dutch turn this into a very special and often hilarious event, one that earns this night the alternative name of *pakjesavond* (parcel evening). These gifts are not bestowed with thought to their monetary value, but rather to help create an atmosphere of anticipation and make the whole affair fun for both children and adults.

Gifts for the older group are usually stacked in some part of the room where the party is held. All gather round as one by one packages are distributed and the ritual of opening them begins. Most packages carry the name of the recipient and are signed with St. Nicholas's name. In reality, wives give to husbands, brothers to sisters, aunts to nieces, and so on, the object being to poke gentle fun, to amuse, and to confuse without disclosing one's identity. Usually a poem accompanies the gift, and here, too, cleverness counts. Many of the Dutch delight in their modest mastery of this art form and could care less about the niceties of meter and form, aiming only to do something original. But to aid those who are too shy or too uncertain of their own skills to compose a poem, professional poem-writers or *sneldichter* will produce to order. Found in department stores in the weeks preceding Sinterklaas Avond, such rhyming specialists will gladly come up with a few lines while the customer waits.

Once the recipient has read and thoroughly appreciated his or her poem the package itself becomes the object of interest. Traditionally, presents are wrapped—or one might say more accurately camouflaged—in some ingenious manner: a pair of earrings buried in a loaf of bread, a whimsical toy encased within a hollowed-out book. Sometimes the gift itself is not even in the package; rather, the recipient finds only the first clue to a chain of leads that must be followed, perhaps to the coal bin or the refrigerator or the rain gutter behind the house, before the gift is discovered.

Meanwhile, the younger children are also engrossed with thoughts of the gifts they will receive. In some households the children once again put their shoes on the hearth, sing their songs, and go to bed, knowing that they will have to wait until morning to find out what the kindly bishop has left them. In others, the good news comes that very evening when the children are allowed to go looking throughout the house for gifts that may be hidden behind the bed, in the bathtub, or under the sleeping dog.

Christmas diorama, Netherlands.

Christmas in Brussels, by Christine Dhan-ani-Lefère, Belgium.

43

Feasting

The Feast of St. Nicholas, as this night's party dinner is sometimes called, may begin with a fine roast chicken or duck, in which father may find his own gift as he carves, and a pudding, in which mother may be surprised to discover something unexpected, too. The Dutch, who have a fine appreciation for desserts all year round, have a number of sweets that they regard as traditional to Sinterklaas Avond in particular. Edible initials called *Letterbankets*, which are a kind of flaky puff pastry filled with almond paste, invariably appear on the table. Sometimes initials at each place show everyone who sits where; in other families, a giant "M"-shaped *Letterbanket*, for Mama, becomes the table's centerpiece. Other treats include honey-based *Taai-taai* cookies, apples and raisin-studded doughnuts called *Oliebollen*, almond-flavored marzipan candy, and *Speculaas*.

Speculaas, or "speculations" as they are known in English, are thin, crisp, spicy, brown-sugar cookies, often flecked with almond bits, that are Christmas favorites in many countries, but nowhere are they more popular than in the Netherlands. Their name is taken from the Latin word *speculum*, meaning "mirror." To make them, the cook presses the dough onto a hardwood plank, which has one large or often many smaller shallow but very decorative images skillfully carved into its surface. Windmills, animals, people, hearts, and Sinterklaas are the most common designs. When the dough is lifted off the board, it comes away with a mirror image of the carving, hence the name. The cookies are then baked to a golden brown.

Both the feast of St. Nicholas and the celebrations of Christmas Day are represented on our Dutch "treat table." The tiny marzipan carrots are symbolic of the carrots (and straw) children leave in their shoes to feed St. Nicholas' horse, should he visit during the night. Other sweets are Letterbankets, Oliebollen, and Speculaas baked in wooden molds similar to those at top right.

45

SPECULAAS

½ cup softened butter
½ cup light brown sugar, firmly packed
1 large egg
2 cups all-purpose flour
2 teaspoons baking powder
½ teaspoon each cinnamon, nutmeg, cloves, and salt

In bowl of electric mixer, cream butter and sugar. Beat in egg. Stir dry ingredients and slowly beat into butter mixture until a soft dough is formed. Shape into a cylinder and chill about 1 hour. Heat oven to 325° F. (160° C). Cut into thin slices and bake on greased cookie sheet about 20 minutes. Cool on rack. Makes about 20 cookies.

OLIEBOLLEN

1 package active dry yeast
1 cup warm milk
⅓ cup granulated sugar
¼ cup butter, softened
2 large eggs
1 teaspoon vanilla
¼ teaspoon salt
3¼ cups all-purpose flour
½ cup dark raisins
1 cup chopped apple
Vegetable oil
Powdered sugar

In large bowl, sprinkle yeast over warm milk. Stir in sugar, butter, eggs, vanilla, salt, and 2 cups of the flour until smooth. Stir in raisins and apple and remaining flour until a soft dough is formed. Cover and let rise until double in bulk, about 45 minutes. Heat about 2 inches vegetable oil in deep skillet to 375° F. (190° C). Stir down dough; drop by tablespoon and fry 3 to 4 minutes, turning once, until golden. Drain on paper towels. Sprinkle with powdered sugar. Makes about 3 dozen.

LETTERBANKETS

1 cup almond paste
¼ cup granulated sugar
1 large egg
Pastry for two 9-inch crusts
1 egg lightly beaten with 1 tablespoon milk

Heat oven to 375° F. (190° C). In small bowl, stir almond paste, sugar, and egg. Chill while rolling pastry. Roll out half pastry about ¼-inch thick into a square. Cut into 2-inch wide strips. On lightly greased baking sheet lay strips to form the letter "M", approximately 10 inches high and 10 inches wide. Press marzipan on top of letter, leaving a ½-inch border on all sides. Roll remaining pastry in similar fashion. Brush border of "M" with egg glaze and place second set of strips over marzipan. Press edges together. Brush surface with egg glaze. Bake about 35 minutes until evenly browned.

MARZIPAN

1½ cups blanched almonds
1 cup granulated sugar
1 cup powdered sugar
2 egg whites

In container of food processor, process all ingredients until smooth. Remove to co'd surface and knead 5 to 6 minutes. Store in refrigerator.

MARZIPAN CARROTS

Marzipan (see Recipe)
Orange good coloring
Green food coloring

Knead about ½ cup marzipan until smooth and pliable. Tint lightly with orange food coloring to resemble carrot color. Knead until evenly tinted. Roll into a thin cylinder and cut into 1-inch lengths. Taper 1 end of each length to form a carrot. Tint green a small amount marzipan; knead until evently tinted. Shape into tiny leaves and attach one to top of each carrot.

Sinterklaas has left gifts for this youngster
to discover on Christmas morning.

Family Christmas in the Netherlands.

47

Giving

Preparations for Sinterklaas Avond and for the Christmas celebrations that follow include decorating the household for the season. The Dutch, like other Northern Europeans, put much creative energy into preparing their homes for the holidays. Everyone in the family contributes, and in the stores Christmas decoration departments bulge with everything from strings of electric lights to tinsel garlands and shiny, fragile glass ornaments. Many families hang an illuminated Advent star in a window four weeks before Christmas, so that some city and village streets twinkle enticingly by night. Garden trees and front doors also come in for their share of lights and decoration. Among the simple but pretty ornaments that children are encouraged to make are pinwheels and beaded garlands.

PINWHEEL

Materials: heavy foil with a different color on each side, mylar or 2 pieces of lightweight foil in contrasting colors glued back-to-back (you can use giftwrap); scissors; metal paper fasteners; colored yarn or thread; pointed tool.

Making a pinwheel

1. Cut 6" (15cm) square from foil, then cut diagonal line from each corner to 1" (2.5cm) from center.

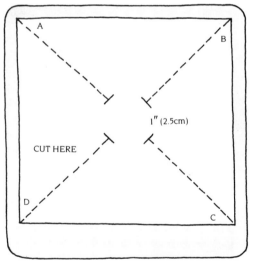

2. Bend points A, B, C, and D over center. Using pointed tool, make holes through points and center and push paper fastener through from front. Open legs of fastener at back.

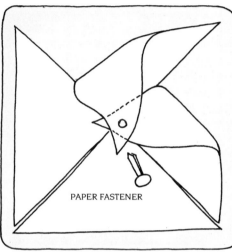

PAPER FASTENER

3. Tie yarn or thread around legs of fastener to make a loop for hanging. You can make larger pinwheels and even a tree-top ornament using larger foil squares.

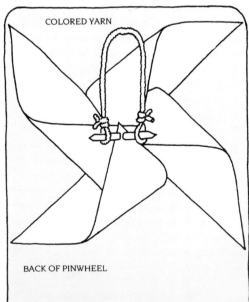

COLORED YARN

BACK OF PINWHEEL

BEADED CHRISTMAS GARLAND

Materials: 3 sizes of round plastic beads with holes: 24 dozen 4mm, 12 dozen 8mm, 3 dozen 12mm, 3 bowls; spool of strong thread; needle with eye small enough to go through beads; scissors. This number of beads will make three 36" (91.5cm) strands which, when tied together, create a garland about 9' (2.75m) long.

To make a really fancy garland, you can use all glass beads (faceted, if you can find them) or a combination of glass and plastic beads. Select 2 or 3 Christmas colors or colors to complement your special Christmas decor.

Making the garland

1. Put each size bead in a separate bowl.

2. Cut 80" (203cm) of thread and thread needle. Knot 2 ends of thread together leaving a tail of about 2" (5cm) and about 38" (96.5cm) on which to string beads.

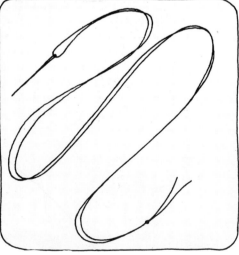

3. String beads to about 2" (5cm) from needle eye. See suggested stringing pattern. Cut thread close to needle and tie knot right next to last bead, leaving a 2" (5cm) tail.

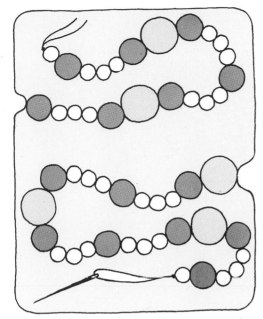

4. Make 2 more strands following same directions.

5. Firmly tie 3 strands close together and cut off excess thread.

Suggested beading pattern: 1 small, 1 medium, 3 small, 1 medium, 1 large, 1 medium, 3 small, 1 medium, so there are not 2 small together, repeat to end of strand.

You can easily make up your own beading pattern, and you can use different sizes of beads. Just remember that if you do, you may have to recalculate the number of beads of each size required to give you 36″ (91.5cm) strands. And don't forget to start each new strand at the point you left off in the beading pattern, to keep the pattern continuous.

When a young child makes a pinweel of shiny colored foil, and it really spins as it is supposed to, it will give off sparkling stars of color. They will dance and mingle with the pride and delight in that child's eyes.

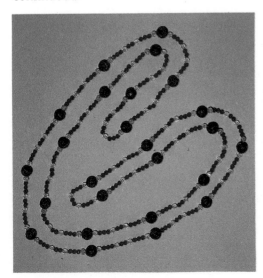

First the popcorn, then the cranberries strung with needle and thread before a warm fire is a Christmas tradition of many lands. Where cranberries do not grow, colored beads create a garland children can make for the family tree.

49

Lucia

Swedes consider their Christmas season to begin late in November on the first Sunday in Advent, when churches and many households light the first of four Advent candles. But it is on December 13th, *Luciadagen* (Lucia Day), that the holiday pace quickens noticeably.

The Lucia for whom this day is named was, according to the most widely accepted legend, a Sicilian Christian who was condemned to death in A.D. 304 for her faith. She supposedly ran afoul of her fiancé's family when she chose to give her dowry to the people of a poverty-stricken village rather than to her in-laws. The prospective groom, deciding that such outrageous behavior could only mean that his intended was afflicted with Christianity, informed upon her to the Roman prefect. She was condemned to burn; but although flames enveloped her pyre, she herself was unharmed. Only when one of her captors plunged his sword through Lucia did she finally die.

This anniversary, which was one of hundreds of feast days subsequently celebrated by Christians everywhere during the year, took on unique significance in the western parts of Sweden during the Middle Ages. One year in early December when a terrible famine gripped the land, Lucia appeared to a Swedish peasant. In his vision Lucia was robed in white, crowned with a circle of lights, bearing gifts of food. This miraculous event was interpreted as an omen of future prosperity, and its celebration coincided with an already long-standing belief that the Norse goddess Freya appeared at about this time each year—the time of the winter solstice—to confer her blessing on the land. The two traditions joined and strengthened each other.

Luciadagen remained a festival of the western provinces, marked by certain rituals associated with the solstice, until the late nineteenth century, when the custom of the eldest girl in the family dressing up to impersonate Lucia first developed. It became a semi-official holiday in this century, one celebrated both within the family and in many shops, offices, clubs, and factories, beginning in the 1920s.

Lucia crowned with candles.

Celebration

Early on the morning of December 13th, Lucia, Queen of Lights, appears in her parents' bedroom, dressed in white and wearing on her head a crown of green foliage and lighted candles. As she carries a tray of special buns and hot coffee, she sings the famed old Neapolitan song "Santa Lucia," only in triple time and with Swedish words. One popular version of the song, to which there are many variations, begins "Mute was the night with gloom: Now hear faint bustling In every silent room, Like pinions rustling. Lo! on our threshold there, White-clad, with flame-crowned hair, Sancta Lucia, Sancta Lucia."

If the family's Lucia has younger sisters, they may follow her, also dressed in white, as though they are her attending angels. Occasionally younger brothers dress up as "star boys" and join in, too, though this again is something of a recent custom. The star boys, who also dress in white robes but wear pointed hats and carry star-topped wands or staves, seem to derive from a different tradition, albeit one also associated with Christmas. Beginning sometime in the Middle Ages, groups of young men, usually students, paraded in costume through the streets singing carols and putting on biblical plays. Often the populace rewarded their efforts with money, food, and drink, which resulted in such giddy and unruly parties that the authorities eventually saw fit to prohibit the young men's activities. Today's star boys appear to be the well-behaved descendants of those earlier mischief-makers.

After the early morning celebration of Luciadagen, Swedes go off to jobs and schools where they continue the day's festivities. In large offices and factories, as well as in shopping centers, it is now customary to elect a young girl to play Lucia, and she passes among her fellow workers bestowing coffee and buns during the morning. Towns and even cities elect their own Lucia, and in Stockholm, where the Nobel Prize winners are usually named on or just before this day, she has the semi-official duty of crowning the winner of the literature prize in formal ceremonies at City Hall. In many places Lucia ends her nameday by leading a candlelight parade through the streets.

The Swedish calendar is alive with holiday events for another full month. First, of course, are Christmas Eve and Christmas, days of family gathering and religious observance. Then comes Boxing Day, or Staffan's Day, named for St. Stephen, when the Christmas Gnome Jultomte distributes gifts. Close on its heels are the festivities of New Year's, Twelfth Night, and, finally, Knut's Day, January 13th. On this day Swedes "sweep out" Christmas for another year. In earlier times, Knut's Day had something of the riotous character of Mardi Gras, with the last of the Christmas wine and brandy being drained at one final climactic party. Nowadays, the wild times are had mostly by the children, for whom Knut's parties are a must. The main event occurs when the children are invited to "turn Christmas out"; they joyfully set upon the tree (which has, of course, already been stripped of its precious ornaments) and plunder remaining candy and cookies. Then, making as much noise as possible and dancing wildly about the house, they drive out any remaining holiday spirits and finally toss the tree out a window or door. That evening, the household adds its well-spent tree to the community bonfire, where its flames join those of dozens of other trees in one last spectacle of the season.

Lucia bringing breakfast.

One of Sweden's Christmas symbols—the beloved orange wooden horse.

Lucia bearing a sheaf of wheat.

"Yule Ram" at Skansen, Stockholm

53

Feasting

On Luciadagen the eldest daughter of the family serves saffron-flavored buns and hot coffee to her parents before they rise from bed. These buns are special to the day and are made in many shapes based upon one or more spirals. Undoubtedly the most popular are Lucia cats (*Lussekatter*), or Devil's cats, which traditionally take the shape of two crossed spirals, with raisins stuck in the center of each coil, much like eyes. Name and imagery are probably holdovers from very ancient times when Norsemen marked the winter solstice with rituals designed to drive off the evil spirits who, they believed, beset the land in the dark days of the year. By displaying an X, which originally symbolized the rays of the sun and only later the cross, householders believed themselves protected from the devil, who often appeared in the guise of a cat. The symbol was incorporated in later centuries as part of the Lucia festival; rather than warding off evil, the X shape and all the other shapes typical of the day's pastries—*Julgat* or single "S" bun, *Gulluagn* or double "S," *Praestens Har* or Priest's Hair, and *Luciakrona* or Lucia Crown—signify the good Lucia's generosity in bringing food to the hungry.

While Swedish families are preparing for Luciadagen, often they are also readying one of the classic dishes of the traditional Christmas Eve dinner. The dish is *lutfisk*, or dried cod. Around or about December 9th, according to country wisdom, the mistress of the house must lay the cod in a bath of slaked lime and soda for slow curing. Fifteen days later, after rinsing it repeatedly, she will steam the lutfisk and serve it with melted butter, white sauce, and boiled potatoes—as the follow-up to a particularly sumptuous smorgasbord. The custom of eating cod on December 24th probably dates from the era of Swedish Catholicism when Swedes prepared to celebrate High Mass at midnight by abstaining from meat at supper. The tradition dies hard, even though many present-day cooks prefer to avoid the arduous and odoriferous task of curing the fish, buying their Christmas Eve lutfisk at the market. And although a number of Swedes profess to dislike the dish altogether, few would feel the dinner complete without it.

Christmas Eve dinner ends with *Rysgrynsgrot*, or Christmas rice pudding. This humble pudding, served hot with ground cinnamon, sugar, and milk or butter, brings forth the poet in everyone, because each person in turn must recite a rhyme before taking the first bite. The pudding is often prepared with an almond or a bean buried inside; whoever gets this portion is destined to marry next or, if already married, to reap some other good fortune. Whoever eats most is going to live longest. These days, most Swedes regard these superstitions as entertaining possibilities, but in earlier times they carried the force of revealed truth.

On Christmas Day a *Jul Skinka*, or Christmas ham, is the great favorite. This dish harks back to the pre-Christian era when the ritual slaughter of a pig, actually a sacrifice to the great god Freyr, marked the Yule, or year's end. Modern Swedes decorate their festive ham with the words *God Yul*, written in white frosting. Translated loosely, this bids all at table a "Merry Christmas."

Throughout the holidays, a favorite party drink is *Julglogg*. The drink, served hot and flaming from a pretty punch bowl, is made with a combination of wine and aquavit, a liquor distilled from potatoes or grain. Flavorings of cloves, cinnamon, raisins, almonds, and lemon peel make the drink as aromatic as it is dramatic. It is easy to prepare, but be forewarned that it is also very potent.

The yeasty saffron-scented plump spiral buns, Lussekatter—the symbols of Saint Lucia's Day, celebrated each December 13th in Sweden—highlight our Scandinavian feast. Our main course is a sliced pork tenderloin with red cabbage and rutabaga. And a cup of glögg to toast "good health" to all.

Christmas dinner with candelabrum.

LUSSEKATTER (LUCIA BUNS)

1 package active dry yeast
¼ cup warm water
⅓ cup granulated sugar
1 cup milk
½ cup butter
1 teaspoon salt
Few threads saffron
1 large egg
4½ cups all-purpose flour
24 seedless raisins
1 large egg beaten with 1 tablespoon
  milk

In large bowl, sprinkle yeast over warm water. Stir in 1 teaspoon of the sugar. Set aside for 5 minutes. In small saucepan, over low heat, heat milk, butter, salt, saffron threads, and remaining sugar just until butter melts. Cool slightly and stir into yeast mixture with 1 egg. Stir in flour to form a dough. Turn out onto a lightly floured surface and knead until smooth and elastic, about 5 to 8 minutes, adding more flour if needed. Shape dough into a ball and let rise, covered, in a lightly greased bowl until double in bulk, about 1 hour. Punch down dough; knead 2 or 3 times. Divide into 12 pieces. Roll each into a 12-inch rope. Curl ends in opposite directions to form an "S" shape. Press a raisin in center of each curl. Repeat with remaining dough pieces. Place 2 inches apart on lightly greased baking sheet. Heat oven to 350° F. (180° C). Let rise until double in bulk. Brush with egg glaze. Bake 20 to 25 minutes until golden brown. Makes 12 buns.

BUTTERED RUTABAGAS

3 medium-sized rutabagas or yellow
  turnips, peeled and cubed
1 tablespoon butter
¼ teaspoon each salt and freshly ground
  pepper
¼ teaspoon ground nutmeg

In a 4-quart saucepan, bring 4 cups lightly salted water to a boil. Add rutabagas; cover and cook until tender, 20 to 30 minutes. Drain. Return to saucepan and toss with spices and butter.

ROAST LOIN OF PORK

1 tablespoon salt
1 tablespoon distilled white vinegar
1 tablespoon Dijon mustard
1 tablespoon freshly ground black
  pepper
1 teaspoon granulated sugar
1 bay leaf, crumbled
3-pound boneless pork loin, tied

Combine salt, vinegar, mustard, pepper, sugar, and bay leaf. Rub over pork loin; cover and refrigerate several hours. Roast at 350° F. (180° C), 30 minutes per pound or until evenly browned and internal temperature measures 170° F. (76° C). Let meat rest 15 minutes before carving. Makes 6 to 8 servings. Serve with Buttered Rutabaga and Red Cabbage with Apples.

GLÖGG

1 bottle dry red wine
1 bottle aquavit
1 cup granulated sugar
1 cup dark raisins
20 whole blanched almonds
6 cardamom seeds
Peel of ½ orange removed with
  vegetable peeler
3-inch piece of cinnamon stick

In large stainless pot over medium heat, heat all ingredients until sugar is dissolved and glögg is hot. Do not let boil. Ladle into glasses or mugs, putting a few almonds and raisins in each.

RED CABBAGE WITH APPLES

2 pounds red cabbage, cored and cut
  into 1-inch pieces
4 medium apples, cored and thinly
  sliced
¼ cup firmly-packed light-brown sugar
1 teaspoon salt
¼ cup red-wine vinegar
¼ cup water
Freshly ground black pepper to taste

In heavy pot or Dutch oven, combine all ingredients. Bring to a boil over high heat. Reduce to a simmer, cover, and cook 30 to 40 minutes, stirring occasionally, until cabbage is tender.

Swedish smorgasbord.

Table ready for the Christmas feast.

Giving

In Sweden, just about everyone in the family joins in making Christmas decorations. The fun begins weeks ahead, often with a day of dipping candles. Candles are such an important part of the festivities that many Swedes take pride in making their own at this one time of the year. The kitchen is the center of operations. The candlemakers press every burner on the stove into service to melt colored tallows, and in bubbling vats the workers repeatedly dip and cool rows of long wicks suspended from sticks. Gradually, dozens of slender tapers emerge and are hung out to harden. The most proficient candlemakers often climax their day's work with a few spectacular examples of their art, multicolored and made in three or more branches.

Costumes must be made, too, both the candle-bearing wire crown for girls who will play Lucia and the cone-shaped, star-studded hats and wands for the star boys who accompany her. The boys' hats, which are fun to wear any time of the year, are made from nothing more than construction paper and foil.

The Swedes also have a tradition of making straw ornaments—stars, hearts, wreaths, angels, fish, birds, people, and animals. The ancients believed that by keeping straw about the house in winter they were paying homage to the spirit of grain, the great life-sustainer. Undoubtedly the most popular of the straw ornaments is the Julbock, or Christmas goat, made of plaited straw, with long horns and a harness of red ribbons. The goat as a symbol, like so much else in the Swedish tradition, derives from ancient Norse mythology, when it was the sacred mascot of the god Thor. The Julbock is to Swedes what St. Nicholas is to many other Europeans—a dispenser of Christmas gifts. Though the Christmas markets in every town offer a wonderful array of these straw ornaments, many families enjoy making their own. All that is required is some straw, some embroidery thread, and a little imagination.

Lastly, many Swedes remember the birds at Christmas with a sheaf of grain, set in the yard if practical or, if not, tied to a pole on the roof. They usually decorate the sheaf with ribbons and may sprinkle it with such special treats as kernels of corn, sunflower seeds, or breadcrumbs. Once believed to insure a good crop in the new year, the sheaf nowadays is simply a gesture of kindness to feathered friends.

HAND-DIPPED CANDLES

Materials: 1 lb. (.45kg) candle wax; 2 oz. (56.7g) beeswax (optional); 6 wicks each 15" (38.1cm) long; two 18" (45.7cm) dowels; two sticks at least 2' (61cm) long; newspapers; chairs; metal or enamel pail at least 12" (30.5cm) deep.

Making the candles

1. To form drip rack, position chairs with backs facing and set the long sticks on chair backs. Spread newspapers on floor between chairs to catch any drips.

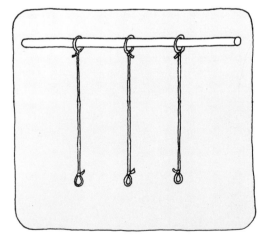

2. Melt waxes in pail on top of stove. Add hot tapwater until wax is floating near top.

3. Tie 3 wicks to one 18" (45.7cm) dowel at 3" or 4" (7.6- or 10.1-cm) intervals (close enough so all 3 can be lowered into the pail of wax without touching the sides or each other). Tie loops at free ends. Repeat with other 3 wicks and other stick.

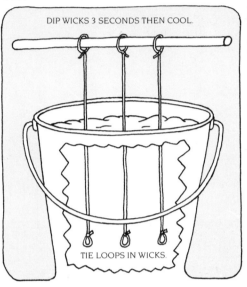

DIP WICKS 3 SECONDS THEN COOL.

TIE LOOPS IN WICKS.

4. Dip wicks to bottom of bucket for about 3 seconds and pull up smoothly. Hang on rack to drip and repeat with other stick of wicks.

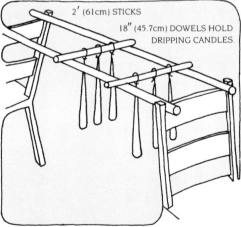

2' (61cm) STICKS

18" (45.7cm) DOWELS HOLD DRIPPING CANDLES

5. When candles are cool, dip again in the same way. Continue dipping and cooling until candles achieve desired thickness, 20 to 25 dippings. If necessary, add more hot water to pail as you proceed. Occasionally straighten candles with fingertips if necessary, and cut away any wax buildup on bottoms. Allow candles to cool thoroughly before removing them from rack.

A Swedish youngster dipping candles.

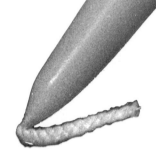

Swedish families make hand-dipped candles to decorate
the house. Some will become part of the glorious crown
the eldest girl will wear on the morning of St. Lucias Day.

Making the popular ornamental goat (julbock) from straw.

59

Advent

In the Christian calendar the month before Christmas is known as Advent, from the Latin term *Adventus Redemptoris*, "the Coming of the Savior." People in many European nations celebrate the season's arrival by taking part in church services, but none quite match the Germans in the intensity and variety of their popular celebrations, which begin on the Sunday nearest November 30th and continue almost uninterrupted til *der erste Weihnachtstag*, Christmas Day.

The custom of observing Advent dates back to the sixth century A.D., when the leaders of the Roman Catholic Church designated the four weeks leading up to Christmas as a time of fasting and penitence, a period of purification that honored the approaching Nativity of the Christ Child. Over the centuries, however, the tone of Advent has changed considerably; now, for most people, it signals a time of joyous preparation and a great deal of eager anticipation for a season filled with more than ordinarily good eating. Towns and cities all over Germany begin their "Lichtwochen" (light weeks) on or about the first Sunday in Advent, stringing bright lights and glittering decorations from lamp post to lamp post and across every store front. The people begin their shopping in earnest at this time, and stores and special Christmas markets entice them with all manner of tempting merchandise. Families who buy their cakes and breads at the local bakery the rest of the year often find themselves at home, making some of the dozens of traditional Christmas cookies and breads that are an integral part of the German Christmas.

Homemade decorations are another much-valued tradition of the season, and families are sure to have their Advent wreaths on display by the first Sunday in Advent. While the candle-lit wreath is Christian in origin, the custom of bringing fir boughs into the home in the darkest months of the year goes back into ancient German history, when evergreens were treated with great veneration because they were thought to contain the spirit of the green life that had gone into hiding with the onset of winter. People in these early days performed magic rites around these evergreen boughs to insure the return of vegetation in the new year. When the Germans became Christianized, beginning in the eighth century A.D., they retained this tradition but adapted it to their new beliefs.

Similarly, the Christmas tree probably originated in these ancient beliefs, though the earliest known use of the tree in connection with Advent and Christmas was in the fourteenth or fifteenth century. At that time miracle plays, especially plays about Adam and Eve, were a part of the season's religious practices. A fresh-cut evergreen, decorated with apples, represented the "Tree of Life" in dramatizing the story of Adam's temptation. Though the custom of religious street theater gradually faded and disappeared, the gaily decorated *Christbaum*, or Christ tree, as it became known, became more and more popular. German families made it a central part of their home observance of Christmas, and over the years they added ornaments besides apples to the tree's decor. At first these decorations were religious symbols: paper roses, representing the Virgin Mary, flat wafers recalling Christ the "host," and stars, symbolizing the Star of Bethlehem. Candles were added probably in the sixteenth century, though folklore has it that Martin Luther introduced the notion of lighting the tree as a way of making his small son remember that the Christ Child was the light of the world.

Kuessnachter Klaeuse. On December 6th in central Switzerland, masqueraders parade in honor of St. Nicholas. The mitre-shaped lanterns on their heads are over 3 feet high.

The *Christbaum* became the secular *Zuckerbaum*, or "sugar tree," beginning in the eighteenth century, when all sorts of edible decorations—cookies, candies, fruits, and sweetmeats—began to crowd its branches. Nuts—some silvered, some gilded—are also favorite decorations; they remind Germans of the old proverb, "God gives the nuts, but one must crack them by oneself," meaning that everyone is confronted by life's mysteries but each must seek to understand them on his or her own.

Celebration

Illustrated Advent calenders are a special delight for children, who learn to appreciate the season by anticipating each of the special days that mark its progress. The most common sorts of calendars are made of cardboard, with dated paper flaps that the youngsters can bend back, one day at a time. Under each flap is a marvelous picture or saying that relates to the story of the Nativity. The last flap, opened on the morning of Christmas Eve (*der heilige Abend*), usually shows a picture of the Christmas tree.

Children soon learn that virtually all of December is a time for celebration. The first big event comes on December 6th when St. Nicholas pays a nocturnal visit to each household, rewarding good children with apples, nuts, and sweets, naughty children with pieces of coal, left in a stocking or boot.

About the same time, families who live in or near one of the large cities take their children to the annual *Weihnachtsmarkt* or Christmas market. The market is devoted to the selling of Christmas foods, ornaments, toys, and other gifts. In Nuremberg, which hosts the most famous and spectacular market of them all, the *Christkindelsmarkt*, the fair is set up in one of the main squares of the old city, right before the 600-year-old Frauenkirche (Our Lady's Church). A huge crèche containing the Christ Child and attended by life-sized figures of Mary and Joseph, the Three Kings, angels, shepherds, and the lowly animals of the field occupies center stage. Around this tableau are clustered dozens of booths selling the same sorts of Christmas treasures that have enchanted German children for generations—nutcrackers, jumping jacks, doll houses, fig and raisin dolls, crib figures, and Noah's arks, to name a few. An especially entrancing item is a "smoking man"

Christmas ornaments.

Outdoor crèche in Switzerland.

doll made in such a way that incense burning inside the doll's body sends smoke curling out through the figure's long pipe.

The opening of the *Christkindelsmarkt* is observed with great ceremony; the mayor and other prominent citizens gather on the steps of the cathedral to greet the Christ Child, who is one of the city's children dressed in white robes and accompanied by two others dressed as golden angels. The child recites the words to an ancient hymn, blesses all those assembled, and declares the market open. Trumpets blare forth from the church gallery as the crowds surge forward into the aisles. Several days after the opening, the rest of Nuremberg's children have an opportunity to play a part in the city's celebration as hundreds of them walk in candlelit procession from the marketplace to Burgrave's Castle on a hill overlooking the northern edge of the city. As the long line threads up the narrow streets to the heights, the children sing Christmas carols. Many of these songs are based upon old German folk tunes—like "Good King Wenceslas"—and the music of such great German composers as Johann Sebastian Bach and Felix Mendelssohn, but now the carols are considered part of the Christmas traditions of Christians all over the world.

The Advent season ends on Christmas Eve when the family gathers at home for a special supper, which traditionally includes carp. Germans have eaten carp on this occasion since at least the Middle Ages, when raising these freshwater fish was an income-producing sideline of many German monasteries. The meal typically ends with a delectable variety of Christmas cakes and cookies. The children then retire to another room to wait while the adults light the Christmas tree and busy themselves with the other necessary preparations. When anticipation has become nearly unbearable, the door opens to reveal the tree and a dazzling collection of gifts, stacked on little tables, a separate table for each person. The family joins hands and sings "O Tannenbaum," a lovely old German folk song that celebrates the Christmas tree's beauty in all seasons of the year. Then everyone falls to opening his or her packages. In most households the Christ Child is nominally credited with bringing the gifts; in some the benefactor is a secular figure known as the *Weihnachtsmann* (Christmas Man). Children, as they get older, come to recognize that their parents deserve a great deal of the credit, too.

Christmas toys and decorations.

Wooden St. Niggi, Baden-Baden.

Parade of Kuessnachter Klaeuse.

63

Our shiny-mahogany roast Christmas goose is garnished simply with sweet preserved cherries. Accompaniments are braised red cabbage and potato dumplings. The Christmas Cake is a Czechoslovakian interpretation of the German Stollen. Our pastry trays are laden with rich buttery confections.

Feasting

Germans pride themselves on the variety and deliciousness of their breads and cookies in all seasons, but Christmas baking is somehow better and more special than in all the rest. Perhaps the most traditional food is *Stollen*, especially the variety that originated in the kitchens of Dresden. *Stollen* are fruit loaves shaped to suggest the crib and the Christ Child wrapped in swaddling clothes. They are flavored with tidbits of traditional Christmas treats—raisins, almonds, currants, and gaily-colored glacéed fruit. Honeyed spice cakes are another specialty, which, though eaten all year round, bring forth the artistry of bakers at this season to an unparalleled degree. Called *Lebkuchen*, meaning "consecrated bread," at Christmastime they are often baked in the form of a gingerbread house, complete with doors, windows, shingles, roof, and chimney, frosted in a way that enhances the wonderful fantasy. Bakers in every region of Germany make gingerbread houses, but those which come from Nuremberg have a special cachet, dating back to the Middle Ages when the Bavarian city was the center of Germany's spice trade with the East. Though the edible edifice will last for months if left alone, in most households the children are allowed to devour the whole thing at the end of Christmas celebrations.

Marzipan, a confection made with almond paste, is also an essential Christmas treat. Although not invented by the Germans—Crusaders found the candy in the Near East and brought it back to Europe—this sweet is uniquely important to the Germans who make it in dozens of shapes, including miniaturized fruits, vegetables, animals, and even elaborate historical tableaux, all colored with a range of vegetable dyes to give them an added measure of realism. The Baltic trading center of Lübeck became the most famous source of marzipan hundreds of years ago and remains so to this day.

Christmas goose.

CHRISTMAS STOLLEN
1 cup dark raisins
½ cup mixed candied fruit
¼ cup chopped citron
¼ cup currants
¼ cup dark rum
1 envelope active dry yeast
1½ cups warm milk
½ cup granulated sugar
½ cup softened butter
2 large eggs
4½ cups all-purpose flour
1 cup chopped blanched almonds

In medium bowl, toss fruit in rum. In large bowl, sprinkle yeast over warm milk. Stir in sugar, butter, eggs, and 2 cups of the flour, until smooth. Work in remaining flour and gather dough into a ball. On lightly floured surface, knead dough 5 to 8 minutes or until smooth and elastic. Knead in drained fruit. In lightly greased bowl, let rise, covered, about 1 hour or until doubled in bulk. Punch down dough; divide in half. Roll each piece into a 12- x 8-inch rectangle. Fold long side of each to within ½ inch of opposite side. Pinch edges. Heat oven to 350°F. (170°C). Place on greased baking sheets; cover loosely and let rise until doubled in bulk, about 30 minutes. Bake 30 to 35 minutes or until browned. Dust with powered sugar. Makes 2 loaves.

POTATO DUMPLINGS
10 slices white bread
½ teaspoon salt
¼ teaspoon freshly ground pepper
1 onion, grated
2 teaspoons fresh parsley, chopped
5 potatoes, peeled and grated
2 large eggs, beaten
¼ cup all-purpose flour

Soak bread briefly in cold water, then drain and squeeze out moisture. Mix with salt, pepper, onion, and parsley. Stir in grated potatoes and the eggs. Form into even-sized patties and coat in flour. Bring a large pot of salted water to a boil. Add patties to water, reduce heat to a simmer, cover, and cook 15 minutes or until cooked through. Makes 6 servings.

BRAISED RED CABBAGE
1 head red cabbage, sliced thin
2 onions, sliced
1 cup dark raisins
½ cup red currant jelly
1 bay leaf
Salt and freshly ground black pepper to taste
¼ pound bacon fat
2 tablespoons red-wine vinegar

Put all ingredients in heavy sauce pot except vinegar. Add ¼ cup water, bring to a boil, cover, and simmer over low heat 1 hour or until tender. Stir in vinegar. Makes 6 servings.

ROAST GOOSE
1 goose, 8 to 10 pounds
3 cups quartered green apples
1 cup sliced onion
3 cloves garlic
1 teaspoon salt
½ teaspoon pepper
Preserved cherries for garnish (optional)

Heat oven to 325°F. (160°C). Stuff goose with apples, onion, garlic and season with salt and pepper. Roast on a rack, 20 minutes per pound until thigh juices run clear and skin is crisp and brown. Baste several times during cooking. Remove to platter. Serve with red cabbage and potato dumplings. Garnish with preserved cherries, if desired.

Swiss Christmas cookies.

A festive seafood dish.

67

Giving

Many families make their own Advent wreaths, using fresh boughs of hemlock, spruce, pine, and juniper from nearby woods. They wire the boughs together in a circle and decorate the wreath thus formed with four candles at the four cardinal points; the wreath is laid flat as the centerpiece on the dining table or sideboard on the First Sunday in the season. On that day the family gathers at dusk to light the first candle, to sing Christmas hymns, and to read from the Bible. (It is also a time for Swiss children to look for an old man, dressed as St. Niggi, to come visit with his pack full of toys for them.) Some families also attach paper stars to the wreath, each star having an Old Testament verse written on one side, a New Testament passage on the other. The children are encouraged to memorize the passages and recite them to the family. The ceremony of marking the progress of Advent is repeated on succeeding Sundays. On the third Sunday, called Gaudete Sunday, the rose candle is lighted as a sign of the joyous season to come.

ADVENT WREATH

Materials: evergreen branches; holly or pine cones if desired; 3 pieces sturdy corrugated cardboard, each 11" (28cm) square; metal ruler; pencil; utility knife; rubber cement; scissors; ¾" (2cm) masking tape; one 4" x 8" (9.8 x 20cm) piece thin cardboard; green poster paint; paintbrush; pointed tool; #30 florist's wire; wire cutters; 1 piece green felt 11" (28cm) square; 1 rose and 3 purple candles 8 to 10" (20.3 to 25.4cm) long.

Constructing the wreath

1. Soak evergreen branches in water 8 to 10 hours to clean and thoroughly moisten them. Shake off excess water before working.

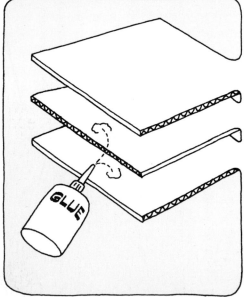

2. Glue cardboard together in 3 layers with corrugations running in alternate directions.

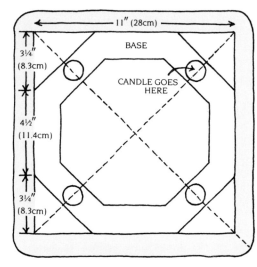

BASE

11" (28cm)

3¼" (8.3cm)

CANDLE GOES HERE

4½" (11.4cm)

3¼" (8.3cm)

3. With ruler and pencil, draw diagonal lines joining opposite corners of 11" (28cm) cardboard square. From each corner measure 3¼" (8.3cm) along both edges and mark those 8 points with pencil dots. Join each pair of dots with a ruled pencil line. Then, using ruler and utility knife, cut away 4 corners of square along these lines to yield 8-sided figure.

4. Come in 1½" (3.8cm) from each of 8 sides and draw lines parallel to outer edges to mark inner edge of wreath. Use ruler and utility knife to cut out center of cardboard square along these lines.

5. Place cardboard base on 11" (28cm) felt piece and draw lines marking outer and inner edges. Using scissors, cut along these lines so felt piece matches base.

6. To position candleholders, mark halfway point (¾" or 1.9cm) along 4 diagonals with pencil.

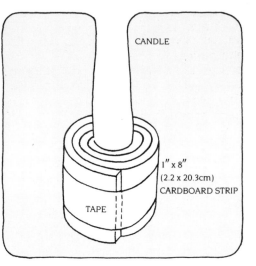

CANDLE

1" x 8" (2.2 x 20.3cm) CARDBOARD STRIP

TAPE

7. From piece of thin cardboard, cut 4 strips 1" x 8" (2.2 x 20.3cm). Loosely roll strip around base of candle and fasten outside end of strip with 5" piece of masking tape. Remove candle and fasten the inside end of the holder with ¼" (.65cm) tab of tape. Repeat for 3 other candleholders.

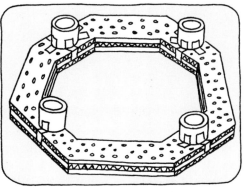

8. Use four 2" x ⅜" (5 x 1cm) tabs of tape to secure each holder in place centered over mark on each diagonal. Paint base and candleholders green and let dry.

9. To attach evergreens, start by using a pointed tool to poke holes about 2" (5cm) apart over the entire surface of the cardboard base.

The tradition of lighting a series of candles one at a time on ceremonial days is common to many cultures. The four candles of the table centerpiece Advent wreath include a rose-colored one which is lighted on the third Sunday of the Advent season.

10. Trim evergreen branches to 4" to 6" (10.2 to 15.2cm) long. Fasten 3 sprigs together with 20" (50.8cm) of wire, keeping sprigs flat and leaving two 8" to 9" (20 to 22.8cm) ends of wire. Lay sprigs on base with stems at center and tips pointing toward edges; secure by sticking wire ends through holes

and twisting them together at back. Continue in this way with small bunches of sprigs, turning wreath counterclockwise until base is fully covered. Overlap stems with sprig tips. If you wish, add holly sprigs using the same wiring method. To add pine cones, attach wires under petals at base of each cone, then push wire ends through holes and twist together.

11. Turn wreath over and cut off all wire ends. Press twisted wires against cardboard and coat back of cardboard with rubber cement. Coat one side of felt with rubber cement, let dry, then press in place against base.·

12. Insert candles and your holiday table centerpiece is ready. Misting the wreath every few days will help keep it fresh and green.

Wigilia

The Poles have always combined religion and family closeness at Christmas time. Gift giving plays only a minor role in the joyous rituals, emphasis being placed instead on making special foods and decorations that capture everyone's attention as young and old prepare for the season. The climactic event is the Wigilia (Feast of Vigil), celebrated in the home on Christmas Eve.

The Wigilia, which derives its name from the Latin word *vigilare* (to watch or keep vigil), has since Christian times been observed as a time of joyful waiting, commemorating the vigil that shepherds kept on the night of Christ's birth. But historians trace its origins to an even earlier age when Poles observed the winter solstice about this time of year. In pre-Christian folklore, the god Saturn conquered darkness and restored the sun, and because he also represented fairness and justice, part of the ancient observance involved people showing forgiveness to one another and sharing foods. Two thousand years and more later, Poles pay homage to this ancient tradition in the *Gody*, the days of harmony and good will that commence at the Wigilia and last until Epiphany, January 6th.

In many families, vestiges of ancient beliefs are apparent also in the custom of making the house uncommonly hospitable at this season. According to legend, wandering spirits roam the land during the darkest days and, just in case there is some truth in the tale, people make provision for the comfort of these lost souls. They leave out a pan of warm water and a bowl of nuts and fruits to refresh possible visitors from the spirit world; and they put away knives and scissors lest the wanderers injure themselves.

Santa Claus greets Polish children.

Celebration and Feasting

The Wigilia meal itself involves rituals that have been handed down over many centuries. Though each region of the country has developed its own unique practices, there is a fundamental similarity among them that derives from the once profound influence of the Catholic Church.

The Wigilia begins officially with the announcement of the first star of the evening. A candle placed at the window for the Christ Child is lighted, and the family assembles to share the feast. By tradition, the table is surrounded by an odd number of chairs, including one for the Baby Jesus. The table, already set, has a bed of straw laid under the white table linen to remind everyone of the straw-filled manger in Bethlehem. On a plate, with money under it to signify a prosperous future, are the symbolic bread and salt without which no household can exist. In the corners of the room are sheaves of golden grain, a silent prayer that the coming year's harvest will be bountiful.

The meal opens with the ritual breaking and sharing of the Oplatek, a large unleavened wafer that has been stamped with scenes of the Nativity and blessed by the parish priest. First the parents break the wafer and share it with one another, embracing and exchanging messages of love. Then mother and father break their pieces again with other members of the family, expressing as they do so the mutual commitment of one for all and all for one. (Family members who are far away will receive pieces of Oplatek by mail—a gesture of continuing family communion.)

The dishes served are also prescribed by custom. They must be meatless in observance of the fast day, and often they number twelve, to symbolize the Twelve Apostles. Ideally, they are prepared with ingredients harvested from the region's own fields, orchards, gardens, woods, and rivers. A clear beet soup filled with mushrooms is the favorite first course, followed by carp and perhaps several other sorts of fish dishes as well as several winter vegetables. Pastries with meatless fillings are traditional, too, including the dumplinglike pierozhki. A grain pudding called kutya always appears, though, with so many delicious alternatives, its eating is more a matter of symbolism than pleasure: ingredients include peeled grain such as rye, wheat, or barley, to remind everyone of the time before there were mills to grind grain; honey, to sweeten the days' labors; and poppy seed, to insure a peaceful sleep. The Wigilia concludes with poppy-seed cake and a compote of twelve fruits, again in honor of the Apostles.

When all have finished, the replete diners rise together and regroup around the Christmas tree where simple, often handmade, gifts await everyone. Midnight finds many families at the Pasterka, the Shepherds' Mass. The next day, Christmas, is spent in the company of close family. Christmas dinner's main course is usually a large ham, Polish sausages, or perhaps the traditional hunter's stew, called bigos, prepared, as its name suggests, from wild game. More traditional Polish communities also celebrate December 26th, "the Second Day of Christmas," in commemoration of the life of St. Stephen. Church services, family visiting, and special meals mark this day, too. Some Poles exchange blessings by tossing a handful of rice at one another, recalling as they do the stoning of the martyred saint.

Szopka (crib) contest in Krakow.

A sleigh ride is always a
winter holiday attraction.

All the children help
decorate the tree.

Goral (highlander) takes part in
carnival near Tarnow.

Highlander Christmas carnival in the Ta-
tra Mountains.

The Wigilia (Christmas Eve) feast includes a borsch (*beet soup*), pierozhki (*dumplings, lower right*), a poppy-seed cake, and kutya, the symbolic grain pudding which contains wheat berries, poppy seeds, walnuts, and honey. The honey sweetens the day's labors; the poppy seeds insure a peaceful sleep.

VEGETARIAN BARSZCZ

¼ head medium-size cabbage, finely
    chopped
2 cups diced celery
½ cup chopped carrot
½ cup chopped onion
1 tablespoon chopped parsley
1 teaspoon salt
1 pound fresh beets, peeled and grated
1 cup sour cream
¼ cup fresh-squeezed lemon juice
1 tablespoon flour
1 tablespoon granulated sugar
1 teaspoon minced garlic

In Dutch oven, place cabbage, celery, carrot, onion, parsley, and salt with 4 cups water. Bring to boil; simmer 30 minutes uncovered until vegetables are just tender. Add grated beets and cook 15 minutes. In small bowl blend remaining ingredients. Stir into soup and bring to boil. Simmer 2 to 3 minutes. Season with salt and pepper, if desired. Serve hot, or chill and serve cold garnished with cucumber slices, if desired.

POPPY-SEED CAKE

4¼ cups all-purpose flour
1 cup warm milk
1 envelope quick-rise yeast
⅓ cup granulated sugar
¼ cup unsalted butter, melted and
    cooled
2 large eggs
½ teaspoon salt
2 cups ground poppy seeds
1½ cups milk
½ cup granulated sugar
¼ cup cornstarch
1 large egg
2 tablespoons softened butter
1 large egg lightly beaten with 1
    tablespoon milk

In bowl of electric mixer beat first 7 ingredients with dough hook at low speed until

flour is incorporated. Increase speed and mix about 5 minutes until dough comes away from side of bowl and is smooth and elastic. Shape into a ball. Put in lightly greased bowl; turn dough. Cover and let rise 1 hour or until double in bulk. Meanwhile prepare poppy-seed filling. In 2-quart saucepan, stir poppy seeds, milk, sugar, cornstarch, 1 egg, and butter over low heat. Bring to a boil and boil 1 minute. Remove from heat and cool to room temperature. Punch down dough. On lightly floured surface roll dough into a 16-x12-inch rectangle. Spread filling over dough, leaving a 1-inch border. Fold dough into thirds at the 16-inch side. Pinch edges; invert onto a lightly greased baking sheet. Heat oven to 375° F. (190° C). Let rise about 30 minutes until double in bulk. Brush with egg glaze. Bake 35 to 40 minutes until evenly browned. Cool on rack.

PIEROZHKI
(POTATO CHEESE DUMPLINGS)

2 teaspoons butter
½ cup chopped onion
1½ cups mashed potatoes
½ cup cottage cheese
½ teaspoon each salt and freshly ground
    pepper
1¾ cups all-purpose flour
1 large egg beaten with ½ cup water
¼ teaspoon salt
Sour cream (optional)

To make filling: In small skillet, melt butter. Add onion and sauté 5 minutes until golden. In large bowl combine potatoes, cheese, sautéed onion, and ½ teaspoon each salt and pepper. Set aside.
To make dough: In medium bowl stir flour with egg, water, and ¼ teaspoon salt to make a smooth dough. Divide into 2 balls. Roll one piece on lightly floured surface less than ¼-inch thin. Cut out ten to twelve

3-inch circles. Place 1 tablespoon filling in center of each. Fold to make a half-moon-shaped dumpling. Pinch edges. Repeat with second ball of dough.
To cook: Heat 3 quarts salted water in large pot to boiling. Cook dumplings in batches in simmering water about 4 minutes after they rise to surface. Remove with slotted spoon to a colander. Drain: keep warm in low oven. Repeat with remaining dumplings. Serve with sour cream. Makes 20 to 24 dumplings.

KUTYA
(WHEAT BERRY PUDDING)

2 cups warm cooked wheat berries
½ cup chopped walnuts
¼ cup honey
2 tablespoons poppy seeds

Stir all ingredients in a medium-sized bowl. Cover and refrigerate at least 2 hours to blend flavors. Makes 6 to 8 servings.

POLISH STUFFED CABBAGE

1½ pounds ground beef
1½ cups chopped onion
½ cup tomato sauce
½ cup raw white rice
2 tablespoons fresh parsley, chopped
1 teaspoon caraway seeds
1 teaspoon each salt and pepper
1 teaspoon dried thyme leaves
1 large green cabbage
¼ cup vegetable oil
1 cup beef broth
Place first 8 ingredients in a bowl and mix well. Remove outer leaves of large head of cabbage and blanch 5 minutes in boiling, salted water until pliable. Drain. Put 2 tablespoons stuffing on each leaf and roll up. Place rolls in a Dutch oven in rows; add oil and beef broth. Cover and cook over medium heat 40 to 60 minutes or until cooked through. Makes 6 to 8 servings.

Crèches competitions are held each year at the foot of the statue of Adam Mickiewicz in Kracow's Market Square.

Carolers call at highlanders' houses.

Giving

Nature's smallest creatures are remembered in Polish folk tales told at this season, and these stories in turn have inspired some of the most beloved Christmas decorations. The spider, or *Pajak*, for example, is supposed to have woven its silken web to keep the Christ Child warm as he lay in the manger, and for this gift of kindness the spider is regarded as a symbol of good luck and generosity. Eggs, blown-out and decorated, are also traditional, as are cornucopia-shaped candy baskets, garlands, stars, and spirals. Except for the eggs, all of these ornaments are made from colored paper and straws. They are hung, along with real apples and other edibles such as cookies, from the branches of the family Christmas tree which is decorated Christmas Eve.

Elsewhere in the house, usually over the center of the dining table or under the ridge beam, Christmas celebrants hang a *Podlaznik*, the tip of a small evergreen hung upside down. The word *Podlaznik* comes from the Polish word "to sneak," and it was customary in rural Poland years ago for young men to go about their villages on Christmas Day offering greetings and snatching kisses from girls under the evergreen bough, the one place and time such forwardness was officially sanctioned. A prettily-made paper mobile is sometimes substituted for the evergreen *Podlaznik*, but the privileges remain the same.

EGG ORNAMENT

Materials: sewing needle; 1 egg; piece of plain blue or green gift wrap 5" (13cm) square; piece of plain red gift wrap 3" (8cm) square; 10" (25.5cm) length of red silk cord; ½" x 6" (1.25 x 15cm) strip of gold paper; sharp, pointed scissors; pencil; pencil compass; household glue; ruler.

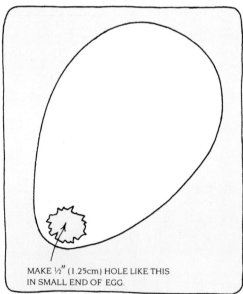

MAKE ½" (1.25cm) HOLE LIKE THIS IN SMALL END OF EGG.

Making the egg ornament

1. Using needle, make series of holes in small end of egg, puncturing yoke. Make an opening about ½" (1.25cm). Shake out egg yoke and white. Rinse egg out with warm water and dry with paper towel.

2. Fold 3" (8cm) square of red gift wrap in half horizontally. Then fold vertically to yield 1½" (4cm) folded square.

3. Along folded edges, draw pencil line consisting of points, curves, and straight sections. Distance from line to fold will vary from ¹⁄₁₆ to ⅜" (.15 to 1cm). Using scissors, carefullly cut along pencil line.

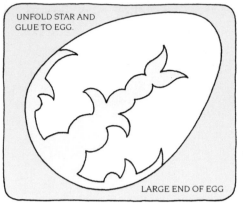

UNFOLD STAR AND GLUE TO EGG.

LARGE END OF EGG

4. Unfold the strip you have cut from the square to reveal a 4-point star with 1½" (4cm) long arms. Glue star to egg, centering it at large end.

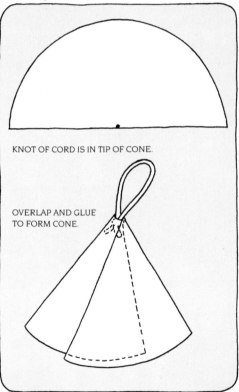

KNOT OF CORD IS IN TIP OF CONE.

OVERLAP AND GLUE TO FORM CONE.

5. On blue or green gift wrap, use compass to draw 4" (10cm) circle and cut out with scissors. Now fold circle in half and cut along fold. Save unused half.

6. Bring 2 ends of silk cord together and tie loose knot. Bend semicircle of gift wrap into cone by overlapping straight edges on either side of center point. Form point of cone around knot of cord. Make base of cone large enough to place on egg as a cap and glue edges of cone together. Then glue cap to small end of egg.

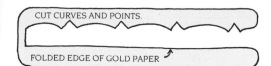

CUT CURVES AND POINTS.

FOLDED EDGE OF GOLD PAPER

7. Fold piece of gold paper lengthwise and cut regular series of curves and points along open edge with scissors. Unfold and glue strip in place around base of cap. Trim off overlapping end.

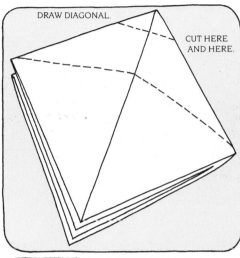

DRAW DIAGONAL.

CUT HERE AND HERE.

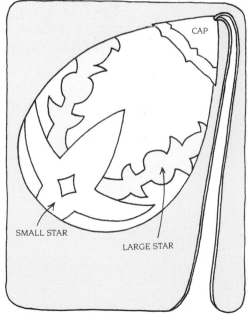

CAP

SMALL STAR

LARGE STAR

8. From leftover blue or green gift wrap, measure and cut 1" (2.5cm) square. Fold twice down to ¼" (.5cm) square. With ruler and pencil, draw diagonal from open corner to folded corner. With scissors, cut out small star as shown. Center over red star and glue in place to fill spaces between red arms.

Chip a hole in the end of an egg, empty it, and decorate it with colored foil to make a traditional Christmas bauble. With care it may be passed down from one generation to another.

Curls of colored paper form an angel for the mantlepiece. This is so simple a task that children will be able to help make many small ones for the tree.

ANGEL

Materials: 14″ x 18″ (36 x 46cm) sheet of colored construction paper; small sheet of white construction paper; sheet of patterned paper or foil gift wrap; scissors; household glue or rubber cement; gold foil; 1½″ (3.8cm)-diameter styrofoam ball; round toothpick; thumbtack; compass.

Making the angel

1. To make robe, set compass point and pencil 5″ (12.5cm) apart and draw semicircle on colored construction paper. Carefully cut out with scissors.

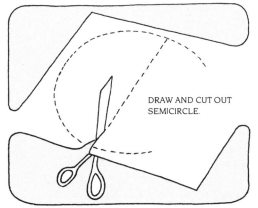

DRAW AND CUT OUT SEMICIRCLE.

2. For hem, draw another 5″ (12.5cm) semicircle on back of gift wrap. then, using same center point, draw 3½″ (8.8cm) semicircle inside 5″ (12.5cm) one. Carefully cut out shape of hem. Line hem up with bottom of robe and glue in place.

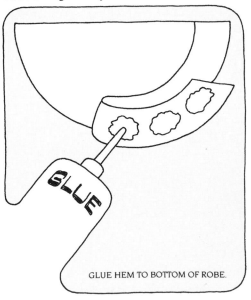

GLUE HEM TO BOTTOM OF ROBE.

3. When glue is dry, form semicircle into cone shape 5" (12.5cm) high and about 5" (12.5cm) across base. Glue overlapping edges.

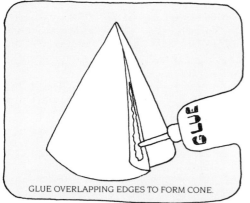

GLUE OVERLAPPING EDGES TO FORM CONE.

4. To make sleeves, set compass point and pencil 3" (7.6cm) apart and draw semicircle on colored construction paper. Cut out semicircle.

5. To make sleeve hem, draw 3" (7.6cm) semicircle on back of gift wrap. Then set pencil and compass 2" (5cm) apart and, from same center point, draw smaller semicircle inside larger one. Cut out 1"-wide semicircle. Line up hem with bottom of sleeve and glue in place.

6. To form sleeves, fold semicircle in half and cut along fold to make two quarter circles. For gluing, fold a narrow wedge along each straight side of each quarter circle to form tabs. Gently bend (do not fold) each sleeve, apply glue to tabs and attach to robe ⅛" (3cm) from point.

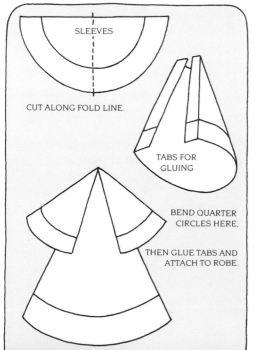

SLEEVES

CUT ALONG FOLD LINE.

TABS FOR GLUING

BEND QUARTER CIRCLES HERE,

THEN GLUE TABS AND ATTACH TO ROBE.

7. To make collar, set compass point and pencil 2½" (6.3cm) apart and draw circle on back of gift wrap. Cut out circle. Make a straight cut from outside to center and form and glue cone just wide enough to cover robe and sleeves. Place collar over robe and sleeves.

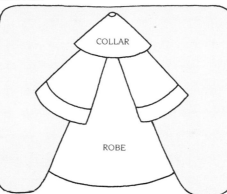

COLLAR

ROBE

8. To make wings, with compass point and pencil 2½" (6.3cm) apart, draw circle on white construction paper. Cut out circle. Make a straight cut from outside to center. Curl edges on either side of cut tightly around pencil.

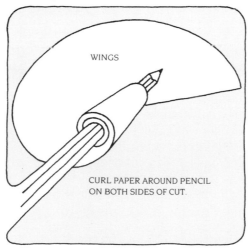

WINGS

CURL PAPER AROUND PENCIL ON BOTH SIDES OF CUT.

9. To make halo, draw and cut out 2½" (6.3cm) circle from gold foil.

10. To make hair, cut from construction paper of desired hair color 2 pieces: 2½" x 1½" (6.3 x 3.8cm) and 5" x 1½" (12.5 x 3.8cm). With scissors, make series of parallel snips to simulate hair strands: about ½" (1.3cm) long snips on one end of 2½" (6.3cm) piece; about 1" (2.5cm) snips at both ends of 5" (12.5cm) piece. Glue 2½" (6.3cm) piece to styrofoam ball so snips form bangs. Glue 5" (12.5cm) piece crosswise just behind bangs to represent hair on top and sides of head.

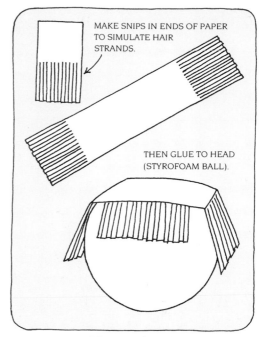

MAKE SNIPS IN ENDS OF PAPER TO SIMULATE HAIR STRANDS.

THEN GLUE TO HEAD (STYROFOAM BALL).

11. To assemble angel, with thumb tack poke hole in bottom of head. Push toothpick into top center point of collar and robe. Place styrofoam ball on collar and secure with toothpick and a drop of glue. Position wings between head and collar and glue in back to collar. Glue halo to back of head. If you wish, paint facial features and cheeks on face of angel.

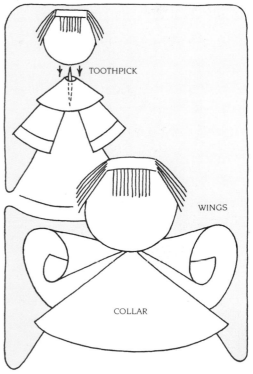

TOOTHPICK

WINGS

COLLAR

Natale

Christmas in Italy is a coming together of two very strong traditions—the ancient Roman and the Christian. For the Romans, the period from December 17th to December 24th was the annual Saturnalia, the time to pay tribute to Saturn, the pagan god of sowing and grain. The week-long festival was a time devoted to indulgence: all businesses, public and private, shut down; executions and military maneuvers were postponed; and slaves, temporarily set free, dined with their masters. Romans entertained themselves night and day with fair-going, unbridled drinking, gambling, and other excesses. Gift giving was traditional, too, the usual tokens being wax candles and little clay dolls, which, it was believed, had been decreed by the gods as practical substitutes for human sacrifices. Saturn himself was expected to carouse with the multitudes; during these days alone every year Romans visited his statue in the Roman forum to untie his bound feet, permitting him to come and go freely. To add to the week's extravagance, one day was set aside for celebrating the birthday of the god Mithras, whom many worshiped as the unconquerable foe of the powers of darkness, showing their appreciation with candlelight processions and great feasting.

Early Christians observed their own Christmas rituals in secret, taking advantage of the spirit of abandon that pervaded the Roman community during the Saturnalia to follow their own beliefs with a minimum of risk. Indeed, it was not until A.D. 320 that the Church of Rome was emboldened to call upon the faithful to proclaim publicly December 25th as Christ's *Natale*, or birthday. Christmas in Italy has been known as Natale ever since, and the celebrations surrounding it are still dominated by the spiritual traditions of the national religion which is, of course, Roman Catholicism.

Museum-quality crèche figures from Italy, arranged in a Nativity scene beneath the Christmas tree erected each year in the Metropolitan Museum in New York City.

Celebration

Nine evenings of special church services, the Christmas Novena, herald the Christmas season in Italy. Worshipers sing Christmas hymns and hear anew the biblical story of Joseph and Mary. Virtually every church and household, and many shops and offices, too, bring forth a *presepio*, or manger, with its surrounding Nativity scene, placing it where all can see. (Often the figures are moved slightly closer to the manger with each day's passing, and the Christ Child appears in the scene only when all have reached the stable on Christmas Eve.)

In 1223 Saint Francis of Assisi introduced the tradition of the presepio in order to make the story of Jesus' birth vivid to his followers. Saint Francis used townsfolk to play the parts of Joseph and Mary, Jesus, the Wise Men, and the shepherds. The notion of dramatizing Christ's birth became so popular that churches all over Italy instituted their own presepios, sometimes with people, but more and more often using small, beautifully carved figures. Some of the presepios we enjoy today include figures that are hundreds of years old, and a popular pastime of many Italians in the days before Christmas is revisiting favorite Nativity scenes.

In addition to setting out the family crèche, Italians typically decorate their homes with sprigs of holly and mistletoe, with candles, and with something unique to their culture—a ceppo. The *ceppo* serves much the same function as does a Christmas tree in other lands, displaying ornaments and gifts for the family.

A cannon shot fired from the Castel San Angelo at sunset on Christmas Eve proclaims the start of the night's holy observances. Families gather for special Christmas Eve dinners, then attend Midnight Mass. The highlight of Christmas Day is another magnificent meal, and St. Stephen's Day, following, is the occasion

Detail from a Nativity scene.

The Magi bearing gifts for the Christ Child.

for visiting friends. People return to work on the 28th, but New Year's Eve and January 1st are marked by revelry and fireworks. Those who are superstitious, and even some who are not, set the pattern for the coming year by doing one of everything pleasurable; popular wisdom has it that by observing this custom, one can be sure to repeat all these delights in the months to come.

Gift giving in Italy is largely a matter of local tradition; the particular date and the form the observance takes vary greatly. In some areas along the Adriatic coast, St. Nicholas's feast day on December 6th is the occasion to give gifts to children, whereas in Sicily they receive gifts on St. Lucia's Day, December 13th. Santa Claus is recognized in some of the larger cosmopolitan areas where he is awaited on December 24th. But most people must wait still longer to receive presents. Some look forward to New Year's Day, an ancient Roman tradition when the practice was to bid good luck in the coming year to friends and family by giving them branches of greenery picked in the grove of the goddess Strenia. Adults accordingly exchange *strenne* and children are visited by *Babbo Natale*, "Old Man Christmas."

But the day most widely devoted to gift giving is Epiphany, January 6th, when the season comes to its official end and a uniquely Italian character named *La Befana* visits many households. Befana is a folk character who, it is said, hesitated to follow the Three Kings on their journey to honor the Christ Child; ever after she has shown her repentance by riding about the countryside on a broomstick, searching for him with her gifts. Though she is forever too late for the *Bambino*, she tries to make up for her mistake by rewarding good children. Just to be sure that she remembers to stop by, children leave her notes and set out shoes or stockings in which she can leave something.

An unusual Nativity scene created from papier-mâché with a painted backdrop portrays the Madonna del Monte and other figures dressed in fabric.

Crèche, Museo di San Martino, Naples, Italy.

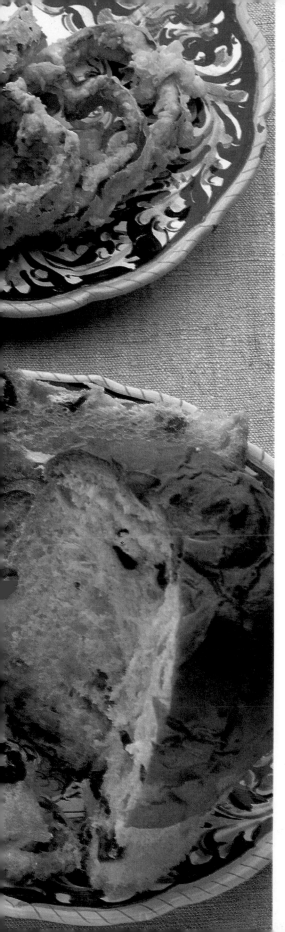

A traditional meatless Christmas Eve meal includes a fritto misto (upper left), batter-fried slices of fresh vegetables. Lentils, a guarantee of prosperity in the new year, are served here with sausage and tomato. And our dessert, a synonym for Italian Christmas, the panettone—a raisin and candied-fruit-studded yeast cake.

Feasting

Christmas foods vary greatly among Italy's twenty regions, but Italians everywhere prepare the meals with great care and ceremony. Christmas Eve dinner, typically served around 7 or 8 P.M., concludes a day of fasting. The customary meatless main course around Venice, Rome, and Naples is *capitone*, or eel, sold live at market and roasted, baked, fried, or steamed. But the people of some other regions prefer cod, clams, or squid. *Frittos mistos*, vegetables dipped in batter and deep-fried, are also favorites on the 24th, along with local pasta and antipasto specialties. The family concludes the meal with sweets and Asti spumante, the Italian sparkling wine, after which the entire household goes to Mass.

Dinner on Christmas Day is served shortly after noon. Often the children of the family prepare for the occasion by writing special letters to their parents, asking forgiveness for misdeeds in the preceding year and promising better behavior in the next. The children hide letters, written in their best penmanship, under their father's plate, and when he "discovers" them he reads them aloud with great solemnity.

This Christmas Day menu, too, varies according to region. North of Rome *capelletti* or, alternatively, *tortellini*, varieties of ravioli, are the traditional choices for the pasta course. The main course is turkey stuffed with chestnuts or perhaps a baked ham, with such customary side dishes as lentils, regarded as a guarantee of prosperity in the new year. Dessert in virtually every part of Italy nowadays includes *panettone*, a type of raised yeast cake filled with raisins and candied fruits. Once a specialty of Milan, it is said to be named for a Milanese baker, Antonio, who set about to improve upon Milan's already delicious pan di Cherubini (Cherub's bread) to win the hand of his beloved. This "Bread of Tony" is the result. Another superb Christmas dessert served chiefly in Sicilian households is *cassata*, a sponge cake with filling of ricotta cheese, candied fruits, almonds, grated chocolate, and rum. Nuts and spicy, honeyed *panforte di Siena* are concluding treats that carry symbolic overtones for all Italians: nuts eaten at this time of year were once believed to ensure fertile farms and families; honey was a gift that was thought to bless the recipient with a sweet future.

FRITTO MISTO

2 onions, sliced into thick rings
2 red peppers, cut into 1-inch strips
2 green peppers, cut into 1-inch strips
1 medium-sized zucchini, cut into thick diagonal slices
1 medium-sized summer squash, cut into thick diagonal slices
3 eggs, beaten in shallow bowl
1¼ cups plain, dry breadcrumbs
2 tablespoons grated Parmesan cheese
2 teaspoons dried oregano leaves
1 teaspoon salt
½ teaspoon fresh ground black pepper
Vegetable oil for frying
Lemon wedges and Italian parsley for garnish

Coat cut vegetables in egg, letting excess drip off and bread lightly in crumbs mixed with cheese, oregano, salt, and pepper. Heat vegetable oil in a heavy skillet over high heat (375°F. or 190°C). Add vegetables a few at a time and fry until golden brown. Lift with slotted spoon onto paper towels to drain. Continue until all vegetables are cooked. Salt lightly and pile onto serving platter. Decorate with lemon wedges and parsley.

ARTICHOKES WITH GARLIC AND OIL

½ cup sliced onion
10 peppercorns
1 lemon, cut into thin slices
4 large artichokes
⅓ cup virgin olive oil
2 teaspoons garlic, minced
¼ cup fresh basil, minced
1 tablespoon fresh-squeezed lemon juice
¼ teaspoon each salt and freshly ground pepper
¼ cup grated fresh Parmesan cheese

Bring a large pot of water to a boil. Add onion, peppercorns, and lemon slices. Boil, covered, 5 minutes. Trim ends off artichoke stems. Put into water, weight with a plate, cover, and simmer 30 to 40 minutes or until stem ends are fork-tender. Remove from water and put in baking pan. Heat olive oil with garlic until garlic is golden. Off heat, stir in basil and lemon juice. Pour over artichokes. Let cool to room temperature. Place artichokes in soup plates and sprinkle with a little of the cheese. Makes 4 servings.

LENTILS WITH HOT AND SWEET SAUSAGE

3 tablespoons olive oil
2 pounds mixed hot and sweet Italian sausage, cut into 1-inch diagonal slices
1 cup onion, chopped
½ cup celery chopped
¼ cup *Pancetta* (Italian belly bacon), chopped
2 teaspoons garlic, minced
1½ cups green lentils
1 cup tomato sauce
1 bay leaf
⅛ teaspoon crushed red pepper flakes

In Dutch oven, heat olive oil over medium heat. Add sliced sausages, onion, celery, *Pancetta*, and garlic; saute 10 minutes until vegetables are soft and sausages lightly browned. Stir in lentils; add tomato sauce, bay leaf, and 2 cups water. Bring to boil. Reduce heat to a simmer; cover and cook 1 hour or until lentils are soft. Remove bay leaf. Makes 4 to 6 servings.

PANETTONE

2 packages active dry yeast
1 cup hot water, 105 to 115°F. (40 to 46°C)
4½ cups all-purpose flour
½ cup unsalted butter, at room temperature
½ cup granulated sugar
3 large eggs
2 teaspoons each grated lemon and orange peel
½ teaspoon salt
½ cup unblanched almonds, sliced
¼ cup chopped citron
¼ cup dark raisins
1 tablespoon melted butter

Bake these attractive holiday breads in 1-pound coffee cans. In large bowl, sprinkle yeast over water. Let sit 5 minutes to dissolve. Vigorously stir in 1 cup of the flour. Cover and let rise about 1 hour until doubled in bulk. In bowl of electric mixer, beat butter with sugar until light and fluffy. Beat in eggs one at a time, then citrus peels and salt. Stir down yeast mixture and beat in with remaining flour, almonds, and fruit. Put into a greased bowl and turn mixture to grease top. Cover and let rise about 1½ hours or until doubled in bulk. Punch down. Divide in two. Grease two 1-pound coffee cans and put one piece of dough in each. Cover with plastic wrap and let rise about ½ hour or until dough rises over tops of cans. Heat oven to 350°F. (180°C). Brush tops of bread with melted butter. Place in oven and bake 30 to 40 minutes until browned and loaves sound hollow when tapped. Cool on wire racks. Makes 2 loaves.

BACCALA (ITALIAN SALT COD)

A 2-pound salt cod, cut into 8 pieces
2 cups fresh tomatoes, chopped
½ cup brine-cured black olives, sliced
¼ cup white wine
2 tablespoons olive oil
6 anchovy fillets, chopped
2 tablespoons capers
1 clove garlic, minced
¼ teaspoon each dried oregano and basil leaves
¼ teaspoon freshly ground black pepper
2 tablespoons snipped fresh chives

Soak cod in cold water 24 hours, changing water every 4 hours. Rinse and pat dry with paper towels. Heat oven to 350°F. (180°C). Put cod in greased 2-quart baking dish. Sprinkle remaining ingredients except chives over fish. Cover with aluminum foil. Bake 25 to 35 minutes or until fish flakes easily with a fork. Transfer to a serving platter; sprinkle with chives. Makes 8 servings.

Detail from Presepio (Museo di San Martin) showing the care with which ceramicists formed these miniatures with needle and clay. Renaissance artists liked to glorify homely scenes by including classic ruins.

Presepio, Museo di San Martino, Naples, Italy. Italian craftsmen were skilled at creating lifelike representations of their world with incredible detail. This is a celebration of food with typical Italian exuberance.

Detail of Mary, Joseph, and the Christ Child.

Giving

The origins of the *ceppo*, the Christmas pyramid whose role in the Italian home is comparable to that of the Christmas tree in Germany, can be traced to the ancient Roman version of the Yule log. This tree trunk, the word for which was *ceppo*, was brought in from the woods at the turning of the year and set afire. Then, with due ceremony, the children—equipped with sticks and blindfolded—were sent forth to do battle with it. The idea was that if they could strike their target, the flaming trunk would yield forth magic. And lo and behold, when their blindfolds were removed, the children witnessed the power of the log's spell—a pile of gifts had appeared before the flaming log. Adults, too, could beat the log and make a wish with some assurance that the wish would be given special attention.

Eventually the *ceppo* went through major changes in its shape and purpose, ceased to be a log and became instead an artificial pyramid with several shelves on which objects and gifts relating to Christmas were arranged. Its pyramidal shape probably was meant to suggest flames rising, or it may have been taken from the shape of Christmas trees. Designing a ceppo challenged the creative genius of artists and artisans, who erected multi-tiered constructions trimmed with colored papers, gold and silver foil, candles, and gilt pine cones. Each tier was then filled with stars, cherubs, bird figures, miniature toys, sweets, fruits, and small gifts, or anything else that seemed suitable to the occasion. The lowest, broadest shelf was often the place where the family displayed its *presepio* (crèche). A few families who own an old, traditional ceppo still bring it out each year for display. Most of the beautiful examples, however, are in museums and are shown in special exhibitions during the holiday season.

MODERN CEPPO

Since Italy has been the inspiration for so many attractive high tech home furnishings, it seemed appropriate to design a modern version of the traditional, ceppo for those who have an apartment or home decor that is sleek and functional.

Materials: 3 fluorescent light sticks, 25" (63.5cm) each, with electrical cords; 1 sheet foam core, 40" x 30" (76.2 x 101.6cm) (available from art supply houses); 1½" (3.8cm) plastic or cloth tape, white; 3 yds. (2.75m) mono filament or strong, clear, polyester thread; small piece of white cloth, sufficient for 12" (30cm) triangle, or white linen or cotton napkin, 10" to 12" (25.4 to 30.5cm) square; 1 pineapple; small Christmas creche figures and assorted greens and ornaments.

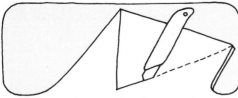

1. Using a sharp utility knife and a metal guide, cut 4 triangles of foam core: 19", 14", 9", and 5½" (48.3, 35.5, 22.8, 14cm).

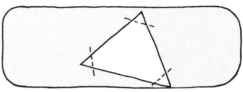

2. Trim 1" (2.5cm) off all 3 points on each of 3 largest triangles only. Then trim the corners so that each tip is 3-sided, as shown.

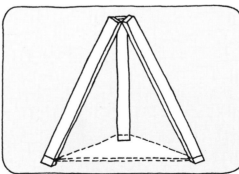

3. Arrange the 3 light sticks so that plugs and cords are at bottom. Ask a helper to hold up the 3 light sticks so the tops touch, forming a small triangle and the bottom ends form a wider triangle, just large enough to fit in the largest triangle of foam core.

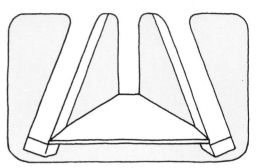

4. Rest the 3 tips of the largest foam core triangle on the plastic edges of the 3 light sticks, at the bottom. Stick a small piece of the white tape under each triangle end and also attach it to the plastic end of the light stick. To give added stability, tie monofilament or strong polyester thread around 3 bottom light stick ends, below 3 points of triangle base.

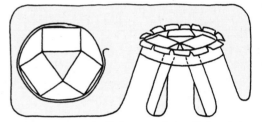

5. Tape around all 3 tops of the lightsticks to bind them together. Leave about ½" (1.3cm) of tape above ends. Snip tape down ½" (1.3cm) at intervals, on all 3 sides, and fold back.

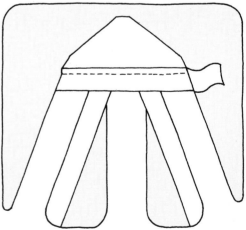

6. Place 5½" (14cm) triangle on top, pressing down gently so it sticks to tape. Make sure it is aligned with triangle at bottom. Cut 5½" (14cm) strips of white tape and place along each edge of top triangle attaching it to plastic ends of light sticks.

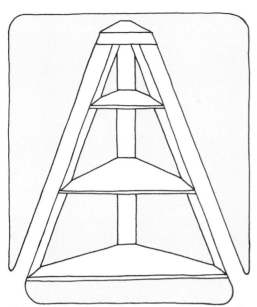

7. Place remaining 2 foam core triangles in positions where they fit snugly, aligning them with top and bottom triangles. Tape into position under each tip.

napkin

tape

8. Arrange cloth or napkin, folded into triangle, on the top triangle and place a pineapple, the sign of hospitality, in the center of it. Arrange creche figures on bottom, and other decorations as desired.

9. Plug in the 3 electrical cords and light up the ceppo by turning the cord switches to the "on" position.

When the holiday season is over, you may wish to disassemble the ceppo and use the light sticks over a desk or in some other area where more light is needed. The ceppo is easily re-assembled if you save the triangular shelves.

The ancient ceppo *springs to light in a contemporary interpretation of neon tubes. Notice the lovely* presepio *(crèche) figures on the bottom shelf and the pineapple, a symbol of welcome and hospitality, on the top.* 91

12 Days of Christmas

In spite of the vast difference in climate between cool Britain and hot Australia, Christmas celebrations in these geographically distant lands are nevertheless remarkably similar. Australians, many of whom trace their origins to the British Isles, have maintained a great many traditional customs; but, of course, they have also added a few unique aspects to the season's observance.

When the first Christmas celebrations were held in the British Isles no one can say for certain, but St. Augustine and forty Roman monks reportedly baptized more than 10,000 believers on Christmas Day in A.D. 598—an event generally regarded as the beginning of modern Christianity in England. By the Middle Ages, Christmas had become the most elaborate and important occasion in a Britisher's year, celebrated with magnificent processions, pageantry, music and dancing, feasting, and merrymaking. Though Christ's birthday provided the central theme, a host of strange and vaguely pagan customs attended the religious observances, holdovers from the traditions of the Saxons, Picts, Celts, Norsemen, and Romans. And even today these early influences show up as local customs that give a special flavor to the British celebration of Christmas.

Mummers, bands of entertainers who dress in fantastic costumes and masks and go about performing ancient folk plays during the Christmas season, offer an especially picturesque example of such customs. The classic mummers' play, which has many variations, tells the story of a heroic St. George, a grotesque dragon, and a half-dozen dangerous adversaries including Captain Slasher and the Turkish Knight. St George kills the dragon, one or more of the other combatants are also slain, and then a comic character known simply as the Doctor steps forward and restores the dead to life; all this takes place to the accompaniment of dancing, singing, and rhyming couplets.

Caroling is another deep-rooted British tradition, going back to the time of the medieval minstrels who went from castle to castle singing for their supper. Nowadays, all sorts of public and private groups go caroling, many of them collecting money for favorite charities as they go. Such songs as "The Boar's Head Carol," the Wassail song, "The Coventry Carol," and "The Holly and the Ivy" have rung through the streets of British towns and cities for literally hundreds of years.

Australians have their own unique custom, called "Carols by Candlelight" and celebrated in virtually every Australian community on either Chrismas Eve or one of the evenings in the week preceding Christmas. This tradition originated in the nineteenth century, when Cornish miners working the copper lode in Moonta, South Australia, began the custom of leaving the mines on Christmas Eve to gather by the light of their "fatjacks" (tallow candles) to sing the carols of their homeland. The inspiration to turn "Carols by Candlelight" into a national tradition belongs to Norman Banks, a Melbourne radio announcer, who was scurrying home from work on Christmas Eve, 1937. Passing by an open window, he chanced to hear a

Christmas parade, Adelaide, Australia.

sweet, small voice singing a Christmas song, and he looked in to behold an elderly lady, candle in hand, seated before her radio singing along with the broadcast. The sight made a deep impression on him, and he launched a drive to get all of Melbourne together for a communal sing-along the next Christmas Eve. Banks persuaded the city fathers to support the idea, and Alexandra Gardens, a park by the side of the Yarra River, was the site chosen. Today hundreds of thousands of Australians, all bearing candles, attend outdoor carol sings in towns and cities and remote cattle stations all over Australia, and many more listen and sing by their radios and television sets.

Celebration

The hustle and bustle of the Christmas season in Great Britain begin well before Christmas and continue with barely a pause to Twelfth Night. The preparation of holiday foods, the sending of Christmas cards (an English notion originally), the decorating of house and church, and the readying of gifts keep all but the youngest family members very busy as the excitement grows.

In the Land Down Under, citizens celebrate the twelve days of Christmas in what is—there—the first month of summer. But the hot weather in no way interferes with the Christmas spirit; Australians decorate their houses and gardens in the fashion typical of a western "white Christmas," some even going so far as to spray artificial snow on their window panes and to dine on steaming plum pudding despite temperatures that may reach 90°F. (32.2°C).

On Christmas Eve, Brititsh youngsters hang up their stockings on the bedpost or by the chimney so that Father Christmas can leave them something. Australian children likewise await Father Christmas or Santa Claus, but they look for the kindly old gentleman to arrive on water skis, in a rowboat, or in an airplane rather than in a sleigh. Children who live in Australia's famed desert Outback are visited by "Santa of the Spinifex" (so named for the scrubby brush that grows along his route), who rides the rails of the Australian Commonwealth Railways System each Christmas to dispense gifts and cheer to those who live in this remote and primitive area where visitors are seldom seen.

In Britain and Australia alike, the family opens presents on Christmas morning and prepares for a big feast, which typically is served just after midday. A Britisher's table gleams with the household's best china and glassware, and at every place is a Christmas cracker, a kind of tube-shaped party favor that produces a loud bang when the paper tabs at the ends are pulled. The meal begins with festive toasts, followed by popping the crackers, which spill forth toys, paper hats, and amusing riddles. Australians may decide to transfer both the elegance and the fun of this meal to an outdoor setting—an option not open to their fellow celebrants in the British Isles.

Not long after the sumptuous meal ends, British families are likely to gather before the television set to hear the annual Christmas speech by Britain's monarch. The custom began in 1932, when families clustered around their radios to hear King George V give special holiday greetings to his subjects all over the world; today his granddaughter, Queen Elizabeth II, carries on the tradition.

In the late afternoon of Christmas, both Britishers and Australians exchange visits with neighbors and family; December 26th, St. Stephen's Day, is likewise devoted to visiting. Long ago people customarily dropped contributions into various collection boxes in the community and distributed the contents to the deserving poor on this day. Gradually this sort of charitable activity was extended to include voluntary tipping of shop apprentices, the chimney sweep, the delivery

Wren boys, Ireland. On December 26th, Wren Day, Irish boys go from house to house singing and dancing, celebrating the day the wren, according to folklore, became the king of birds because it could fly the highest. The boys receive a few coins in appreciation for their antics.

boy, the milk maid, the postman, and so on. Boxing Day, the popular name for St. Stephen's Day, is so called because of this custom. In Australia, Boxing Day is the occasion for many sporting events, all of which are attended by throngs of enthusiastic spectators.

More celebrations follow at New Year's. In Scotland and Ireland, where Christmas tends to be marked with more solemnity, the end-of-the-year doings are particularly joyous. *Hogmanay*, as New Year's Eve is called in Scotland, is a night of fun and revelry. Children go door to door demanding hogmanay or oatmeal cake, and parents celebrate with cakes and *athole brose*, a cold brew made with whiskey, heavy cream, honey, and oatmeal. When the bell tolls announcing midnight, the head of household makes a grand gesture of opening wide the front door to let the Old Year out, the New Year in. Then the family anticipates the arrival of the "first footer." By tradition, good luck requires that the first foot to cross the threshold on New Year's Day belong to a dark-haired man, perhaps to distinguish him from the fierce Norsemen who more than once invaded and pillaged the land. To be sure that no person who is light-haired, female, flat-footed, blind in one eye, or otherwise different from the ideal first footer has a chance to cross the threshold first, and thereby cast an evil spell on the house, most families prearrange for a visit, moments after midnight, from someone who fits the proper description.

Christmas parade, Adelaide, Australia.

Irish children light a candle in the window on Christmas Eve.

Color lithograph and paper-lace, anonymous, ca. 1870/80. Victoria and Albert Museum, London, England.

Carols by candlelight.

The Carol Singers, by Pamela Cornell, U.K.

Village Snowball Scene, anonymous, nineteenth century, U.K.

97

Feasting

In the Middle Ages, a roast pig or, better yet, a roast boar dominated the Christmas dinner table in the more prosperous households of England. This impressive dish was brought into the dining room to great fanfare and acclaim. Typically dressed with an apple in its mouth and rosemary sprigs in its ears, the festive porker demonstrated its symbolic origins, which are rooted in the time of the Norsemen, who annually sacrificed to Freya, the goddess of fertility, in return for her restoring the sun and springtime. Other dishes only slightly less exotic followed: swan, partridge, larks, peacock, and roast goose.

Over the centuries, the excess characteristic of the British Christmas dinner has been tempered considerably, and roast goose—or, less frequently, suckling pig—is perhaps the only consistent survivor from the list of medieval main dishes. But several old-time desserts have kept their traditional place in the holiday feast, among them mince pie, plum pudding, and that hearty bowl of hospitality called the wassail.

Mince pie, according to food historians, is appropriate to Christmas because it symbolizes in its spicy filling the gifts of the Magi, in its latticework crust the hayrack above the manger, and in its traditional shape—for centuries it was made in a loaf pan—Christ's manger. Though some may find this symbolism farfetched, it is worth noting that during the Protestant Reformation in England the very baking of such a Christmas pie was viewed as an act of popery; the baker was suspected of being Catholic and was quite likely to be arrested. The delicious pie prevailed nonetheless, though it did undergo some changes. Once made with chopped beef and suet, as well as preserved and dried fruits, nuts, spices, brandy, and rum, it is more likely to be made without the meat these days.

As for plum pudding, it is told that Daga, the god of plenty in ancient Celtic lore, created the forerunner of this Christmas cake when she prepared to celebrate the winter solstice by making a pudding of the best fruits, meats, and spices that could be found on earth. By the fourteenth century the pudding, or porridge as it was then, had become an essential part of the holiday feast, though it was served at the beginning of the meal. It made its way to the dessert course by stages, becoming thicker and sweeter along the way.

Tradition once attended its making, which was supposed to commence on "Stir up" Sunday, the first Sunday in Advent, when the opening words of the Collect began "Stir up, we beseech Thee, O Lord...." English housewives, duly instructed, spent the rest of the day doing just that. Two methods of preparation were considered proper, depending upon the particular recipe used. One could steam the pudding in boiling water and age it for several weeks or, quite the opposite, store the batter and then steam the pudding on Christmas morning. Despite its name, plums are seldom if ever used today in plum pudding, although before raisins became a staple of the English kitchen, prunes (dried plums) were included.

"Was hal!" ("Be hale and healthy!") an Anglo Saxon saluted as he raised his cup to his companions. By the Middle Ages, the words had come to describe a hearty drink of hot spiced ale. Slices of buttered toast were often floated atop, leading to the custom now described as "raising a toast." Wassail is typically served during the Twelve Days of Christmas, a time of general merrymaking and visiting among friends and family. People who are not so fortunate as to have hospitable friends may make some new ones by going wassailing, or Christmas caroling. According to custom, in exchange for a few well-sung verses they hold

Our "sweet" table offers (clockwise from upper left) plum pudding and hard sauce, toast triangles to accompany the traditional Wassail Bowl, miniature mincemeat tartlets, and a festive Australian Pavlova, a meringue shell topped with whipped cream and sliced strawberries and kiwis.

out their portable wassail bowls for a refill. In some rural parts of England a night's singing can end in a farmer's orchard where a last chorus is rendered for the fruit trees to insure a bountiful harvest in the New Year.

PLUM PUDDING

2 cups fine cake crumbs
½ pound suet, finely chopped
1 cup granulated sugar
4 large eggs, lightly beaten
½ cup brandy
¼ cup heavy cream
1 tablespoon each grated orange and
    lemon peel
2 tablespoons fresh-squeezed lemon juice
1 cup all-purpose flour
½ teaspoon each ground cinnamon,
    nutmeg, and allspice
¼ teaspoon ground mace
1 cup chopped pecans
1 cup currants
1 cup golden raisins
1 cup diced dried figs
¾ cup diced dried apricots
Mint leaves for garnish

Thoroughly butter two 1-quart steamed pudding molds. Mix cake crumbs, suet, sugar, eggs, brandy, cream, orange and lemon peels, and lemon juice in large bowl until smooth. In medium bowl mix flour and spices. Stir into cake crumb mixture. Stir in remaining ingredients except mint leaves until blended. Scrape into prepared molds. Cover tightly with aluminum foil. Place molds on rack in large kettle or pot. Pour in boiling water halfway up sides of molds. Cover pot and steam over low heat about 4 hours. Add more water if necessary. Unmold puddings onto cake plates. Serve with Lemon Mint Hard Sauce (see recipe) and garnish with fresh mint leaves, if desired.

LEMON MINT HARD SAUCE

⅓ cup unsalted butter
1 cup powdered sugar
¼ cup heavy cream, scalded and cooled
    to lukewarm
1 tablespoon chopped fresh mint
2 teaspoons grated lemon peel
1 teaspoon fresh-squeezed lemon juice

In bowl of electric mixer, cream butter and sugar until light and fluffy. Gradually beat in cream and remaining ingredients. Serve with Plum Pudding. Makes about 1 cup.

PAVLOVA

3 eggs whites
Few drops lemon juice
¾ cup granulated sugar
2 cups whipped cream
1 pint strawberries, sliced
3 kiwis, peeled and sliced ¼-inch thick
(1 passion fruit, if available)

Heat oven to 175° F. (79° C). Beat egg whites and lemon juice until frothy. In bowl of electric mixer, beat in ½ cup of the sugar gradually until the mixture is stiff and glossy. Fold in remaining sugar by hand. Line a baking sheet with parchment and draw two 8-inch circles thereon. Spread meringue evenly over circles, pulling up slightly at edges. Bake about 3 hours until meringues are dry and lift easily off the parchment. Cool on rack. Place one meringue on serving dish and cover with whipped cream, leaving a 1-inch border Arrange sliced fruit decoratively over cream.

(This recipe makes two 8-inch meringues. One may be stored in a cool dry place in an air-tight container at least 1 month.)

Passion fruit is the special flavor of the truly authentic Australian pavlova. However, the dessert is also delicious with other fruit combinations, such as those suggested here.

MINCEMEAT TARTLETS

1 cup all-purpose flour
1 tablespoon granulated sugar
¼ teaspoon ground nutmeg
¼ teaspoon salt
6 tablespoons cold butter, cut in small
    pieces
Yolk of 1 large egg
1 tablespoon plus 1½ teaspoons brandy
1 tablespoon cold milk
2¼ cups prepared mincemeat
1 egg lightly beaten with 1 tablespoon
    milk

In container of food processor, process flour, sugar, nutmeg, and salt 10 seconds. Add butter and process until mixture resembles oatmeal. In small bowl, whisk yolk, brandy, and milk. Add to flour mixture and process just until mixture forms a mass. Shape into ball and chill, wrapped in plastic wrap or foil, about 1 hour. Heat oven to 375° F. (190°C). On lightly floured surface, roll pastry ¼-inch thick. Line twelve 3½-inch tart pans with dough, reserving scraps. Fill each tartlet with about 3 tablespoons mincemeat. Reroll dough scraps; cut into lattice strips and criss-cross 2 strips over each tar-

Christmas dinner spread, England.

tlet. Brush with egg glaze. Place 2 inches apart on baking sheet; bake 20 to 30 minutes until filling is bubbling and crust is golden. Makes 12 tartlets.

WASSAIL BOWL

3 cups granulated sugar
12 cups ale or beer
2 cups dry sherry
1 teaspoon each ground cinnamon, ginger, and nutmeg
1 lemon, cut into thin slices

Put sugar into a large punch bowl. Stir in remaining ingredients except lemon slices. Float lemon on top and serve. Serve with toast triangles, if desired. Makes about 4 quarts.

Christmas boar's head.

101

Giving

Quite apart from the traditional Christmas tree, the British "deck the halls" with a lavish hand, using several sorts of greenery, each of which carries mythic associations. Mistletoe, for example, dates from the time of the Celtic Druids, who regarded this plant as both a protection against witchcraft and a bringer of good luck. By the Middle Ages mistletoe was included in a Christmas contrivance called the "Kissing Bough," which was the precursor of the Christmas tree.

The Kissing Bough consisted of a semicircular frame of willow branches or wire, suspended from the ceiling and covered with greenery. Ribbons, apples, candles, and perhaps even a few tiny gifts were worked into the design, and a sprig of mistletoe hung from the bottom. Candles were lit for the first time on Christmas Eve and thereafter every night until Twelfth Night. Family and friends sang carols in its shadow and children danced beneath it, and every time a woman passed by, she risked a kiss from any gentleman in the room. The excuse for such behavior, then and now, was that a kiss delivered under the sacred mistletoe was a pledge of friendship and good will.

Christmas greens used in the Kissing Bough are often made from a combination of two or more aromatic plants, including evergreen boughs, holly, laurel, ivy, and rosemary. Holly is a reminder of Jesus' crucifixion, the prickly leaves reminiscent of the crown of thorns, the red berries of the drops of blood shed. Holly is also said to protect a house against fire and storms; some believe that if it is picked from a bunch that first hung in church, it carries the blessings of holiness and happiness to its new surroundings.

Laurel and ivy as festive decorations are ancient Roman imports, the first much used to celebrate victories, the second to symbolize Bacchus, the god of wine. Rosemary is a strictly Christian symbol, recalling the old legend in which Mary hung out the Baby Jesus' swaddling clothes to dry on a humble rosemary bush. When the rosemary imparted its beautiful smell to the garments, God ordained that rosemary should ever after have a place of special honor in the plant world.

KISSING BOUGH

A traditional Kissing Bough combining some or all of these kinds of evergreens is relatively easy to construct.

Materials

1 wire coat hanger; 2 yds. (1.8m) aluminum wire; 4 yds. (3.7m) red cord; darning needle and red thread; 5 candles [preferably European style, of beeswax, approx. 3" (7.5cm)]; aluminum foil; 4 small apples—red Macintosh or similar; twigs and small branches of evergreens; 4 sprigs of mistletoe, live or artificial.

1. Take apart the wire hanger and bend so it is shaped into a double half-circle.

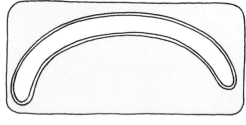

2. Bend and criss-cross the aluminum wire under and over the two hanger wires, covering the entire frame twice.

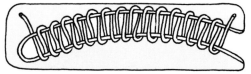

3. Cut the red cord into two pieces. With one piece, leaving a tail at about 3" (7.5cm), knot the cord to the frame at point A, pull it across and knot it again at point AA. Then knot the 3" (7.5cm) tail and the long portion of cord in the middle, as shown. Repeat with the other end at points B and BB. Repeat sequence with second piece of cord, knotting this time at points C and CC and D and DD.

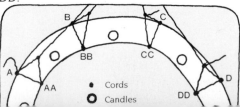

4. Hold up cords and let frame hang freely. When cords are taut and frame is level, tie knot about 3" (7.5cm) from top. Resulting loops are used to hang up Kissing Bough.

5. Cut out 10 stars of foil.

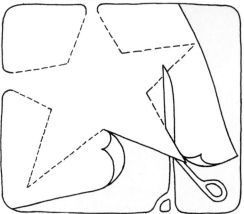

6. Place 2 stars on top of each other and center candle in middle. Press foil up around candle bottom, making a holder and drip catcher. Separate a wire space at one end of frame and fit candle base, with foil, snugly inside. Repeat until all candles are in frame at positions shown.

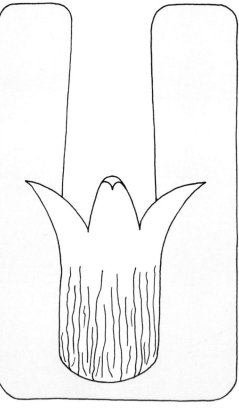

7. Hang frame so it swings about 3" to 4" (7.5 to 10cm) above a counter or table top. Thread a darning needle with red thread. From below frame, tie end of thread to one of the red cords. Push darning needle and thread into one of the apples directly through middle of core. Let apple rest on counter or table top as you tie a piece of mistletoe to bottom of apple, using the red thread that was pulled through. Repeat process for remaining 3 apples.

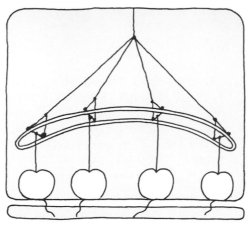

8. Hang frame higher so apples swing freely. Arrange small branches and twigs of evergreen by poking them into frame from bottom and top. When frame is completely covered, the Kissing Bough is ready to hang wherever it will attract the most action.

Apples and wild mistletoe hang from the evergreens in the "Kissing Bough." Delicate tapers glow in a delicately balanced candelabrum beneath which a Christmas kiss may be stolen.

Las Posadas

Christmas—*Las Posadas, Navidad,* and *Dia de los Tres Reyes*—throughout most of Latin America is a season of bright flowers and brilliant nights. Though Central America is entering winter at this time of year, the weather is warm and dry for the most part, and in those countries in the Southern Hemisphere summer is just beginning. The celebrations, the holiday foods, the songs, though they vary from country to country according to the influence of each country's indigenous Indians, all share a strong Latin heritage dating from the arrival of Roman Catholicism four hundred years ago. Christmas is, then, very much a religious holiday centered around the age-old story of the *Nacimiento,* Christ's birth. Here we focus on Mexico and Venezuela to describe some typical festivities commemorating this most important holiday.

Celebration

In Mexico, the joyful observances begin on December 16th. From that evening until the eve of Christmas, processions of family and friends go from house to house, by prearranged invitation, to take part in one or another of the countless *posadas,* or "lodging" parties, that provide the central social events of the season. Part amateur theatrical, part religious ceremony, the *posadas* dramatize the nine-day journey of Mary and Joseph to Bethlehem.

In preparation for the season of *posadas,* the people of Mexico decorate their houses and apartments with festoons of greenery and build small altars atop which they place tiny nativity scenes representing the crèche, the stable, the shepherds, their flocks, and the expectant Mary and Joseph. Then, just as evening falls, the members of each *posada* gather to recreate the ancient pilgrimage. Two children, carrying figures of Mary and Joseph, lead the procession. In towns the throng may go from house to house, but in cities they may wind through apartment house corridors or even from room to room. At each door, they pause to sing that they are tired and cold and in need of shelter for the night. They ask for lodging.

Other members of the *posada* take the role of inhospitable innkeepers. Opening the door just a crack, they refuse to take in the strangers, and the party moves on. Finally, they reach the door of the evening's host's house. When Joseph identifies himself and tells of his family's long journey and of the imminent birth, the owners respond, also in song, saying, in effect, "Then you are welcome in our humble home, and may the Lord remember us all when our souls go to heaven!"

The ritual is by now a very old one, and though every adult has repeated it a great many times, each *posada* holds mystery and excitement. When at last the

Celebration of Three Kings' Day in Mexico.

pilgrims are invited in, a great cheer goes up. The candlelit procession enters and gathers around the decorated altar to kneel reverently in prayer. Then the evening's fun begins. Fireworks, delicious sweets and fruits, dancing, and a *piñata* filled with small treats for the children are traditional ingredients of the party.

The *posadas* are repeated for nine evenings, the last on Christmas Eve. This evening of joyous climax is the most solemn and elaborate of them all. For the first time, two members of the procession step forward as "godparents." They carry a figure of the Baby Jesus, which they lay gently in the manger. Other participants light candles set in a row around the altar, and everyone joins in singing hosannas.

Christmas Eve ends with the *Misa de Gallo*, or Mass of the Cock, at midnight. After the service, everyone spills out into the streets, fireworks explode overhead, bells ring, and a joyous clamor sounds all over town. In some communities a special parade, with floats and *tableaux vivants* representing biblical scenes, provides a spectacular finale to the public part of Christmas. Finally, in what is more often than not the middle of the night, everyone returns home for a special dinner.

December 25th is typically a quiet family day, which is understandable—after the very late night that has just passed. In the days that follow Mexicans continue the joyous season by attending special bullfights, *pastores* (miracle plays), and fiestas. December 28th is the day of *Los Santos Inocentes* (Holy Innocents), a time for children to play practical jokes and tricks. Gift giving does not occur until January 6th, the *Dia de los Tres Reyes*, Three Kings Day, when the Magi are said to return and to give presents to children, as they once did to El Nino Jesus. Just to be sure that they do not escape notice, many children prepare for this night by writing letters to the Magi, listing their good deeds and suggesting gifts that they hope to receive.

In Venezuela, *posadas* are not traditional, but the season begins, nevertheless, on December 16th when families bring their *nacimientos*, more often called *pesebres* here, out of safekeeping and arrange them in the most prominent part of the living room. Venezuelan *pesebres* range from the most literal depictions of the nativity scene to some rather unorthodox displays that combine modern-day electric trains and cartoon figures with the traditional shepherds, pilgrims, Wise Men, and the Holy Family.

Going to one or more of the nine *Misas de Aguinaldo*, the 4:30 A.M. Christmas carol services, is a bracing custom that most Venezuelans observe. Firecrackers explode and bells ring to call worshipers from bed in the predawn hours. *Aguinaldo* is the Venezuelan term both for a carol and for a gift, which gives some notion of the spirit in which the joyous singers lift their voices to the Niño. The last of the Christmas masses takes place on *Nochebuena de Navidad*, Christmas Eve. Families go together to the late night *Misa de Gallo* and then home to a huge and fancy dinner. Some young bloods steal away from their own kith and kin to serenade the young ladies. Though the idea is to sing Christmas carols, more often than not the songs take on more earthy, romantic themes.

The Day of the Holy Innocents, December 28th, is marked much as it is in Mexico as a day for playing jokes on friends. It is also the day on which the Church recalls the martyrdom of the young children who were slain by Herod in retribution for Christ's birth. Lastly is the *Dia de los Tres Reyes*, January 6th, when a child awakes to find the straw left the night before by his bed gone and gifts delivered in its place. This, the youngster knows, is the work of the Magi and their hungry camels. Lo and behold, when the child goes to the mirror, he finds a smudge of black on his cheek. Balthasar, King of the Ethiopians, kissed him as he slept!

Christmas display of lights in Brazil.

Aymará Indian children playing Christmas games, Bolivia.

Young Ecuadorian girl singing a joyous Christmas carol.

Colorful costumes for the "Gran Poder" festival, La Paz, Bolivia. Villagers from all over the country arrive before dawn to participate in a gala parade that features banners, musicians, and—especially—dancing. The celebration can be traced to the time of the ancient Mayans and Incas.

Nativity, appliqué by Leonor Cardenas, Colombia.

108

A tribute to the sun made of yarn on plywood, bees-wax, by Ramón Medina Silva.

Brazilian crèche.

Sun mask constructed of papier-mâché and cigarette package gold strips. Colombia.

Feasting

In Mexico, the traditional sweet of the Christmas season is the *buñuelo*, a large, flaky fritter or doughnut that is usually eaten with cinnamon-flavored syrup. The fritters are served on a cheap pottery plate, and part of the fun of eating a *buñuelo* is smashing the plate to the ground afterward, a devil-may-care gesture that is supposed to bring good luck. *Buñuelos* can be found in every marketplace at this time of year, but they are especially popular in Oaxaca, a district known for its pottery. The *buñuelo* eating and plate breaking start in earnest on December 17th, when the city turns out to honor its patron saint, the Virgin of Solitude. The custom picks up speed on or about December 23rd, the *Noche de los Rábanos* (Radish Night), when citizens tour the open-air displays of the annual radish-carving contest. (This event, which is a showcase for the finest carvers in the district, inspires extraordinary flights of skill and fantasy in the making of images out of Oaxaca's famed giant rosy-red radishes; nativity scenes, political satires, and replicas of bullfights are just some of the subjects likely to be exhibited this night.) Finally, this orgy of doughnut consumption reaches its peak on Christmas Eve, as everyone comes away from the last *posada* of the season and joins a *calenda*, a procession of fellow communicants heading joyfully toward Midnight Mass.

Of course, many other excellent Mexican treats are abundant during the Christmas season, including *tamales* covered with a chocolate sauce, *revoltijo*, a dish of prickly pear, shrimp, and potatoes seasoned with rosemary and chili, and *ensalada de Nochebuena*. This last dish is a robust salad, made with mixed fruits, beets, and peanuts, eaten as part of the Christmas Eve feast, perhaps as an accompaniment to stuffed turkey.

Venezuela also has its unique Christmas specialties, and *hallacas* head the list. *Hallacas* are a variety of cornmeal pie stuffed with pork, chicken, plus all sorts of delicious flavorings, and steamed in wrappers of plantain or banana leaves. The most popular holiday dessert at this time is *dulce de lechosa*, a very rich preservelike pudding made with candied papaya. Superb candies, called *turrons*, are also a must. Chewy confections, they resemble the French nougat and the Italian *torrone* in consistency and flavor and are thought to have been introduced to Venezuela by Spanish missionaries centuries ago.

Our Caribbean Christmas dinner features traditional Pasteles from Puerto Rico. Plantain leaves are stuffed, folded and tied in neat packages and boiled. Opened, each reveals a spiced filling of pork, ham, plantain, tanier, olives, capers, chick peas and raisins. The dessert, heart-shaped Tembleque, is a sweet coconut pudding garnished with fresh mint leaves and an amapola flower.

111

PASTELES

Dough
2 medium-sized green plantains
3 pounds taniers (a type of yam)
2 pounds all-purpose potatoes
1 cup milk
½ cup solid shortening, simmered 30 minutes with 3 tablespoons annatto (achiote) grains and strained
2 teaspoons salt
Pinch sugar

Stuffing
1 pound cubed pork
2 tablespoons olive or vegetable oil
½ pound cubed cured ham
2 cups chopped onion
1 tablespoon minced garlic
2 cups chopped green pepper
1 jar (4 ounces) chopped pimentos
3 tablespoons chopped Spanish olives
3 tablespoons capers
1 tablespoon minced fresh coriander (cilantro)
½ cup tomato sauce
1 cup cooked chick peas
3 tablespoons dark raisins
½ teaspoon salt
Freshly ground pepper to taste

Wrappers
1 pound plantain leaves
Kitchen string

To make dough: In container of food processor or blender puree, in batches, plantains, taniers, and potatoes with the milk until smooth. Transfer to a large bowl. Stir in shortening, salt, and sugar. The dough will be reddish-orange. Put into a plastic bag and refrigerate.

To make stuffing: In large, heavy skillet, heat olive oil over medium heat. Add pork, ham, and onion and cook 5 to 10 minutes or until lightly browned. Add garlic and cook, stirring 1 minute. Add green pepper, pimentos, olives, capers, and coriander. Cook 5 minutes. Add tomato sauce. Let simmer 20 minutes or until pork is tender. Add chick peas and simmer 5 minutes. Stir in raisins and salt. Season with pepper.

To assemble: Wash plantain leaves and pat dry with paper towel. Cut into pieces about 11 x 8 inches. Grease lightly with olive oil. Spread about ½ cup dough into the center of each leaf, covering an area 7 x 4 inches.

If dough is too stiff, add a little water. Using a slotted spoon, put about 3 tablespoons of the stuffing in center of dough. Fold sides of leaf in, then fold ends in to form a package. Tie securely with a long piece of kitchen string. Bring a large pot of lightly salted water to a boil, add Pasteles, and simmer 45 minutes, covered. Makes 12 Pasteles. (Do not eat plantain leaves.) Serve Pasteles with sliced tomato, avocado, and onion salad.

TEMBLEQUE

1 large coconut
1 quart boiling water
½ cup cornstarch
⅔ cup granulated sugar
1 teaspoon vanilla extract
¼ teaspoon salt
Mint sprigs or fresh flowers for garnish (optional)

Lightly moisten the inside of a 5-cup heart-shaped mold and place in freezer. Crack coconut open. Loosen meat from shell; scrape off brown skin with vegetable peeler. Cut meat into ½-inch pieces. Put in blender or food processor with 1 cup of the boiling water and process until smooth. Transfer to a large bowl. Stir in remaining 3 cups boiling water. Let stand 1 hour. Strain through cheesecloth-lined strainer and squeeze to release all moisture. Measure liquid. You should have 4 cups. If necessary add water to equal 4 cups. Pour into a 3-quart saucepan. Stir in cornstarch, sugar, vanilla, and salt until smooth. Place over low heat and cook, stirring constantly with a wooden spoon, about 40 minutes or until thick and pudding-like. Remove from heat and pour into prepared mold. Let cool about 10 minutes. Refrigerate until firm. Unmold onto attractive cake plate and garnish with fresh mint or flowers, if desired.

ENSALADA DE NOCHE BUENA

¾ cup olive oil
3 tablespoons orange juice
2 tablespoons red-wine vinegar
1 tablespoon chopped fresh coriander
½ teaspoon salt
3 cups cooked, cubed beets
2 cups orange segments

2 cups peeled, chopped jicama
2 cups chopped fresh or canned juice-packed pineapple
3 sliced bananas
2 cups shredded iceberg lettuce
½ cup sliced unblanched almonds, toasted
Seeds from 1 pomegranate
Fresh coriander springs (optional)

Fresh coriander and jicama may be found at Mexican specialty shops. Stands selling oriental fruit and vegetables are also likely to carry fresh coriander. Be warned, it is very pungent.

In the bottom of a large bowl, mix first 5 ingredients. Add beets, oranges, jicama, pineapple, and bananas. Toss gently to mix. Cover and refrigerate 1 hour. To serve, mound in center of a large, festive platter. Arrange shredded lettuce around salad. Sprinkle beet mixture with toasted almonds and pomegranate seeds. Garnish with coriander, if desired. Makes 8 to 10 servings.

BUÑUELOS

2 cups all-purpose flour
½ teaspoon baking powder
¼ teaspoon salt
½ cup milk
1 large egg
Vegetable oil for frying
Raisin-Wine Sauce (see Recipe)

In large bowl, stir flour, baking powder, and salt. Stir in milk and egg to form a dough. Knead lightly until smooth. Divide into 15 balls. Roll each very thin between sheets of wax paper. In large skillet, heat oil to 350° F. (180° C). Fry dough, several pieces at a time, 3 to 5 minutes, turning once until golden. Drain on paper towels. Serve with Raisin-Wine Sauce (recipe below). Makes 15.

RAISIN-WINE SAUCE

⅓ cup dark brown sugar, packed
½ cup dry red wine
½ cup dark raisins
½ teaspoon ground cinnamon

In medium size saucepan, heat all ingredients to a boil over medium heat. Simmer 5 minutes until lightly thickened. Spoon over hot buñuelos.

Candlestick, anonymous folk art from Oaxaca, Mexico.

Christmas in Panama, by Nancy Dupuis de Munévar, Panama.

Nativity, anonymous mola, Panama. Illustration from the book Molas, Folk Art of the Cuna Indians, by Ann Parker and Avon Neal.

113

Giving

Children all over Latin America play a Christmas game that centers around the *piñata*, a fragile earthenware or papier-mâché container filled with nuts, candies, and other goodies. Nowadays, *piñatas* are just for fun, and their images are either humorous—a fat bull, a funny-faced head, a Santa Claus—or related to holiday symbolism in some way—a star, perhaps, or a fantastical bird. They are decorated all over with gaily colored streamers, tissue paper fringes, sparkles, and more. But the *piñata* was originally a religious symbol representing the conflict between Good and Evil. The *piñata* of old was made in the form of Satan, dressed in various shades of red and other brilliant colors to lure innocent mortals. And the treasures inside were symbols of the temptations which Satan places before humankind. The game then was a morality play in which blindfolded combatants, wielding sticks and operating on blind faith, sought to destroy Evil.

In the modern game, the *piñata* is hung overhead, just out of easy reach. One by one, children are blindfolded, handed a stick, and given three chances to hit the target. Just to be sure that the game is as difficult for the older children as for the younger ones, the *piñata* is often suspended in such a way that an adult can raise and lower it to suit each player's skill. When some lucky child finally scores a solid hit and the *piñata* shatters, spilling its treasures, everyone makes a mad scramble for the floor to grab up as much as possible. In Mexico piñatas are climactic ends to every *posada*. Elsewhere, the game may be part of the Christmas Eve family get-together or some other celebration of the season.

PIÑATA

Materials and tools

Round balloon, inflated size 10" to 12" (25 to 30cm); newspaper; 1 cup (140gm) flour; 2 cups (.5l) water; large bowl; pie tin; pencil compass; 5 sheets construction paper at least 15" x 15" (38 x 38cm); aluminum foil; rubber cement with dispenser and brush; scissors; 2 pieces heavy cord, 20" (50cm) and 6' (185cm); 1" (2.2cm) masking tape; package of 20" x 30" (50 x 75cm) sheets of brightly colored tissue or crepe paper party streamers; large empty food can; 8" (20cm) piece of string; assorted candies; small toys.

To make Star Piñata

1. Select a balloon that will inflate to 10" to 12" (25 to 30cm). Blow it up and tie it. Tear, do not cut, sheets of newspaper along grain into 2" (5cm)-wide strips. For paste, mix flour and water in large bowl and pour into pie tin.

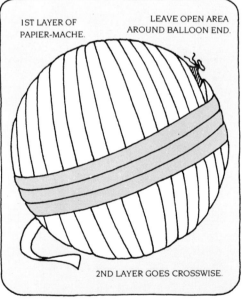

1ST LAYER OF PAPIER-MACHE.
LEAVE OPEN AREA AROUND BALLOON END.

2ND LAYER GOES CROSSWISE.

2. Draw strips through paste, then through fingers to remove excess, and wind around balloon. Apply more paper strips and continue winding until balloon is covered. Add a second layer, running the strips at right angle to the first layer. Continue until you have 4 layers. Set papier-mâché ball aside to dry thoroughly, up to 4 days. Then deflate and remove balloon.

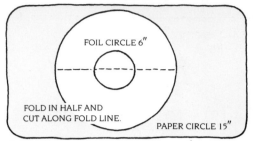

FOIL CIRCLE 6"
FOLD IN HALF AND CUT ALONG FOLD LINE.
PAPER CIRCLE 15"

3. To form star points, use pencil compass to draw 15" (38cm)-diameter circles on construction paper and cut them out. With pencil compass, mark three 6" (15cm)-diameter circles on aluminum foil and cut them out. Rubber cement 1 foil circle to 1 paper circle with centers lined up. Repeat for other circles.

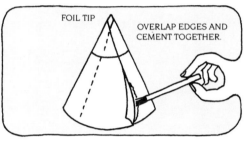

FOIL TIP
OVERLAP EDGES AND CEMENT TOGETHER.

4. When cement is dry, fold 1 circle in half and cut along fold to yield 2 semicircles. Repeat for other circles. Bend 1 semicircle into cone, foil side out, overlap edges a little, and rubber cement edges together. Repeat to form 4 more cones.

5. Use scissors to make ½" (1.25cm)-deep cuts ½" (1.25cm) apart around bases of cones to form tabs. Spread tabs out, evenly space cones on a line around ball (but not over opening) and tape tabs to ball. Now make a hanger by securely taping ends of 20" (50cm) cord to front and back of star so that center of cord is about 2" (5cm) above opening.

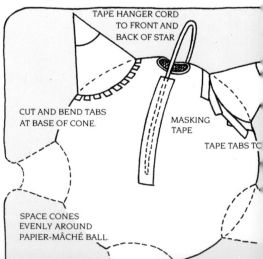

TAPE HANGER CORD TO FRONT AND BACK OF STAR

CUT AND BEND TABS AT BASE OF CONE.

MASKING TAPE

TAPE TABS TO

SPACE CONES EVENLY AROUND PAPIER-MÂCHÉ BALL.

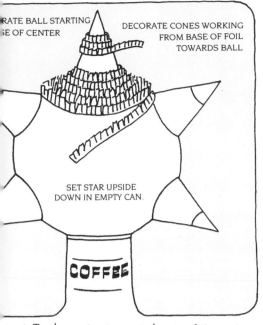

DECORATE BALL STARTING
E OF CENTER

DECORATE CONES WORKING
FROM BASE OF FOIL
TOWARDS BALL

SET STAR UPSIDE
DOWN IN EMPTY CAN.

COFFEE

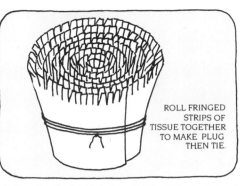

ROLL FRINGED
STRIPS OF
TISSUE TOGETHER
TO MAKE PLUG
THEN TIE.

8. To plug hole, tightly roll 2″ x 30″ (5 x 75cm) strips of fringed tissue into a stopper large enough around to fit snugly into hole. Tie stopper with string ½″ (1.25cm) from unfringed side.

9. Fill star with candies and toys, insert stopper and attach 6′ (185cm) length of cord to hanger and to ceiling fixture so piñata is low enough that a child can reach it with stick.

6. To decorate star, cut sheets of tissue into 2″ x 30″ (5 x 75cm) strips. Make fringe by snipping a series of cuts along 1 edge of each strip. Cuts should be about 1½″ (4cm) deep and ¼″ (6mm) apart. Turn star upside down and support it with empty can while decorating. Brush rubber cement along unfringed edge of tissue strip and cement it fringe-side-up horizontally around ball at base of center cone. Apply a second strip below first, overlapping to hide glued edge. Continue until ball is covered. In the same way, decorate cones but leave foil tips uncovered. Work from bottom of foil toward ball.

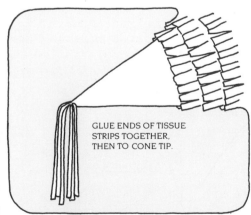

GLUE ENDS OF TISSUE
STRIPS TOGETHER,
THEN TO CONE TIP.

7. For tassels, cut a 4″ x 10″ (10 x 15cm) tissue strip, then cut it into forty ¼″ x 4″ (6mm x 10cm) strips. Make tassel by gluing tips of 8 strips together and then to point of each cone.

A star that lights winter celebrations throughout the world is the symbol for a Mexican piñata. It is made of paper and, as every child knows is filled with treats that crash to the floor when they break it open.

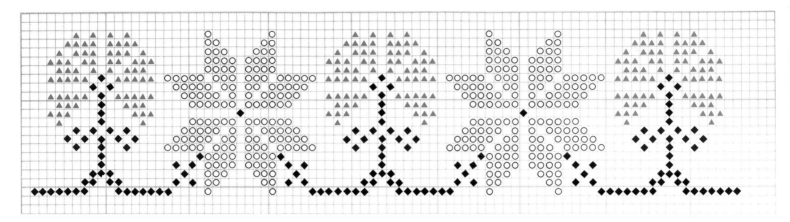

NEEDLEPOINT OR CROSS-STITCH SAMPLER

FROM A SAMPLER, PUEBLA, MEXICO

This Sampler motif may be executed in either needlpoint or cross stitch.

Materials: double- or single-mesh canvas for needlepoint or #18 even-weave material (preferably linen) in neutral or pastel color for cross-stitch; yarn for needlepoint: pearl cotton, regular cotton, 3-ply Persian-type wool, or linen; yarn for cross-stitch: silk or linen about same texture as material; package of assorted blunt-end needles #18 to #22; heavy scissors; small, pointed scissors; ruler; permanent marker; masking tape. Optional: thimble; felt-tip coloring pens; hoop or frame; graph paper.

Designing the sampler

You can follow chart as shown, or pattern can be repeated, enlarged, or reduced. You can use suggested yarn colors, or select different ones.

Selecting background material and yarns

Once you have decided on size of finished sampler, you are ready to purchase the appropriate amounts of background material (canvas or even-weave) and yarns. #5 canvas is recommended for quick-point, #12 for regular needlepoint. When estimating amount of background material, allow at least 2" (5cm) extra all around for blocking and mounting. To estimate amount of yarn for needlepoint, figure 1 yard (92cm) of yarn for each square inch, then allow some extra. Test sample of yarn on background material before buying large amounts.

1. Put masking tape around all 4 edges of background material to prevent fraying.

2. Mark center and outline of actual size of finished piece on background material with permanent marker.

3. If you are repeating pattern, or changing suggested color scheme, rechart pattern on graph paper using felt-tip coloring pens. Always start center of a repeat in center of background material.

4. Thread each color yarn in its own needle. Work with threads not more than 18" (46cm) long.

5. As you start to work, remember never to knot yarn. Fasten it by weaving it in and out on back of work. And should yarn get twisted, hold material up in the air and let threaded needle hang down. The yarn will unwind.

6. Follow chart carefully as you proceed on sampler.

7. When you have finished working sampler, check it carefully. Look for missing stitches by holding it up to a light. If you find any, fill them in. Make sure all threads are carefully secured on back, and clip very long threads. Pull any loose stitches from front to back and secure with another thread.

Blocking the needlepoint sampler

Note: light pressing with a dampened pressing cloth will usually be sufficient for a cross-stitch sampler.

1. Dip clean sponge into mild soap solution and go over entire back of sampler until it is thoroughly dampened. Do not press or rub.

2. Lay sampler face up on a board with enough give to push in tacks or pins. Insulating wall board lined with graph paper covered with plastic works well.

3. Using graph paper as a guide, tack dampened sampler down at ¼" (6mm) intervals with rustproof pins or tacks.

4. When sampler is completely dry, remove it from board. Repeat procedure if sampler is still not square.

Mounting the sampler

You can do your own framing if you have the expertise. Otherwise, purchase a ready-made frame or have your work mounted by a professional.

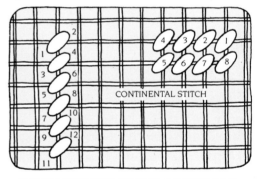

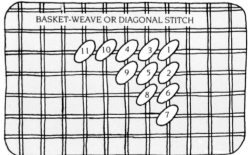

Nativity, Maria de Kantorowicz, Colombia.

Christmas

Because of the rich cultural mix in both the United States and Canada, Christmas celebrations there seem nearly endless in variety. Some families, even though they are second, third—or perhaps even fifth—generation North Americans, observe the holidays by returning to their roots and the traditions of their ancestors. They decorate their houses, prepare festive foods, and follow Christmas rituals with as much Old World flavor as might be found in the lands their forebears left. Other North Americans celebrate Christmas with a distinctly New World twist, picking and choosing among the many customs and practices they see about them to tailor their holiday observances precisely to their own tastes. Still others celebrate a combination of the Christian Christmas and some non-Christian holiday, such as Hanukkah, Diwali, or Kwanzaa, which falls very near to Christmas.

Christmas in North America, then, defies precise description, but the spirit of good will and joy and family closeness so pervades the season that no one can avoid it, whatever one's personal beliefs. Every town has decorated trees, displays of lights, and busy shops. Depending upon the particular groups who settled there over the centuries and the climate, it is also likely to have at least one holiday practice that is peculiarly its own.

Take, for example, the hundreds of *luminarias* that light up the Christmas skies in many southwestern U.S. communities. These ingenious devices, made of small brown paper bags half-filled with sand and holding small candles inside, are set out as nighttime decorations in some communities where Mexican-Indian Americans predominate. As best anyone can discover, the custom evolved from the *farolitas*, paper lanterns that Mexicans carry during the *posadas* and the bonfires made of piñon boughs that southwestern Indians traditionally burn in homage to the spirits of the sky at this season. Beautiful to look at and inexpensive to make, *luminarias* have been adopted as outdoor Christmas decorations by many "Anglos" as well.

Christmas celebrations in North America got off to an early start when Christopher Columbus's flagship, the *Santa Maria*, shipwrecked on the shores of Hispaniola on Christmas Eve, 1492. Saved by the local Indians, he invited them to dine with him on Christmas Day and, for good measure, named his first settlement there La Navidad, meaning Christmas. In the next two centuries, those areas settled by the Dutch, the Swedes, the Spanish, and the Anglicans of England marked the day as their compatriots back in the Old World did. But Puritan New Englanders were forbidden by their church elders to observe Christmas because the Bible made no specific reference to such an observance. One suspects, also, that all that celebrating and socializing may have seemed, to that somber and escetic group, to set a dangerous precedent. Many other sects—the Congregationalists,

A child, whose snowsuit almost matches Santa's, looks as if she is thinking hard about the delicious question that Santa Claus traditionally asks, "And what would you like for Christmas, little girl?"

Presbyterians, Baptists, Methodists, Mennonites, and Quakers among them—disapproved of the holiday, too. Only when the United States became an independent nation and religious issues were specifically separated from political ones did Christmas become the national secular holiday that it is today.

Though people of German heritage brought the custom of Christmas trees to the New World perhaps as early as the late eighteenth century, Christmas trees did not come into general use until the mid-nineteenth century when the English put their stamp of approval on the notion. Poinsettias, plants native to Mexico, became the traditional flower of Christmas in the late nineteenth century. They were introduced to the North by Joel Poinsett, amateur botanist and U.S. ambassador to Mexico. Captivated by Mexico's *Flor de la Noche*, which blooms forth every December with a brilliant display of traditional Christmas colors—green and red—he began growing cuttings in his gardens in South Carolina. Other gardeners soon followed suit.

As for Santa Claus, this magical bringer of gifts was a home-grown product. The Dutch had their *Sinterklaas* with his white horse and the Germans of Pennsylvania their *Christ Kindl* (or "Kris Kringle," as many pronounced it). But the St. Nicholas or Santa Claus who is alive and well today sprang from the imagination of a New York scholar, Clement Moore. Dr. Moore published a lengthy ballad entitled "Twas the Night Before Christmas..." in 1822 and thereby created the mythology of a kindly old man who toils all year long making toys up at the North Pole in preparation for one night's visit to children all over the world. The sleigh, the eight tiny reindeer, their curious names, were all invented on the spot for the entertainment of Moore's own offspring, but publication in a local newspaper set them on their way to immortality. To this day, parents still delight in reading the poem to their children on Christmas Eve, one of the many ways in which traditions pass virtually unchanged from generation to generation.

Celebration

In a secular sense, the Christmas season begins in the United States right after Thanksgiving Day, which is always the last Thursday of November. Towns choose the weekend following Thanksgiving to erect Christmas trees and hang special lights in the streets, and stores welcome Santa Claus to their toy departments. One of the country's major department stores, R.H. Macy's, holds a mammoth parade on the streets of New York, and children all around the country spend a part of Thanksgiving morning watching the spectacle on television and anticipating the exciting Christmas season about to begin.

From then until December 25th, the excitement grows, as virtually every American finds his or her normal routine altered by preparations for Christmas. Everyone's head is abuzz with shopping lists and party plans and, for the more fortunate, there are Christmas concerts and plays to go to, as well. One entertainment that ranks at the very top of the list for many urban parents and children is Tchaikovsky's *Nutcracker Ballet*, which is performed in dozens of cities around the country at this time of year.

House decorations begin to appear around the first Sunday in Advent. A popular example is a wreath at the front door. New Englanders are especially fond of putting a single candle—the electrified sort these days—in each of their windows. In suburban neighborhoods without a conservative bent, families often illuminate their front lawns with elaborate scenes of Santas and reindeer and other Christmas symbols. Christmas is also a time for buying and preparing special foods, both

Decorating the Christmas tree with a traditional homemade star, U.S.A.

Quebec winter carnival, Quebec, Canada.

Urban display of Christmas lights, Canada.

Hanging stockings—especially homemade ones that can be used year after year—by the fireplace is traditional in both the United States and Canada. Santa Claus has filled these colorful stockings with goodies for the entire family. Larger gifts are usually placed under the Christmas tree, but here they are stacked on the mantlepiece.

to give as gifts to friends and neighbors and to serve as part of entertaining at home. For those who plan to celebrate an old-fashioned Christmas according to their particular ethnic heritage, Christmas often means making a shopping trip to their old neighborhood, where holiday breads and cakes and candies are still prepared and sold.

A Saturday may be set aside for finding the perfect Christmas tree; some families insist on driving out into the country where "cut-your-own" tree farms encourage those with a spirit of adventure to fell their own evergreen with their own hands. Some households decorate the tree early in December, coincident with the beginning of Advent; others save the tree-trimming for late Christmas Eve, when the children are already in bed. When it comes to tree-decorating styles, North Americans are as eclectic in their tastes as they are in the foods they eat. Some families like a "natural-looking" tree, with strings of popcorn and cranberries and homemade ornaments of straw; others go for the glitter of tinsel and glass balls and dozens of colored lights. Still others decorate their trees with Old-World ornaments, or design "theme" trees, all in one color or with ornaments particular to the family's hobbies.

For weeks before the holidays, church, school, and social groups gather to practice Christmas carols and to prepare special pageants. The mailbox fairly bursts with Christmas cards (a tradition originally British) which daily bring new messages of greeting from far-off friends and relatives. And plump Santa Clauses in red suits, snowy beards, and black boots seem to be everywhere—in stores

Scene from a Christmas drama, U.S.A.

Manger scene from a Nativity pageant, U.S.A.

listening to the special requests of excited youngsters, along busy city streets collecting donations for the poor and needy, on television reminding shoppers that the days 'til Christmas are running out. Because most schools close a few days before Christmas and remain closed until after New Year's, Christmas is also a time for families to travel to see distant relatives.

The actual Christmas celebration begins on Christmas Eve. Many Protestant churches hold special candlelight services during the evening, and Roman Catholic churches offer Midnight Mass. Meanwhile, children are engrossed with preparing for Santa's late-night arrival. They set out their stockings—by the fireplace, on their bedroom door, or on the bedpost. A note for Santa wishing him well, a snack of cookies and milk, and perhaps some carrots for the reindeer are all considered wise and sensible ways to stay on Santa's list of deserving boys and girls.

Christmas morning starts in many households before dawn as youngsters, unable to control their excitement any longer, run to see what Santa has left. These gifts are likely to be of the games and goodies sort. Later in the day, the whole family gathers around the tree to exchange more substantial gifts among themselves. "Doing the tree" in some households happens even before breakfast, while everyone is still in nightclothes; other families delay the exquisite pleasure until after breakfast or even until late in the day, when members of the extended family arrive to share Christmas dinner. The day ends with almost everyone exhausted. Fortunately, the routine of ordinary school and work life will not resume again for many people until after New Year's Day.

Family Christmas carolers, U.S.A.

Santa Claus, by Gail Bruce, U.S.A.

Christmas Out-of-Doors, by Rodman Pell, U.S.A.

Child placing the Christ Child in the center of the Nativity scene, U.S.A. 125

Feasting

Our North American tableau: The scent of pine permeates the Christmas table. First course is a spiced pumpkin soup. The tourtière (upper left) is a traditional Canadian pork pie served at Réveillon, garnished here with a pastry-dough maple leaf. Dessert is a cream-topped Canadian maple pie and a mug of frothy eggnog sprinkled with fresh-grated nutmeg.

Like America itself, a fruitcake is a mixture of many ingredients and traditions. Almost all recipes call for a flavoring liquid of some sort, frequently spirits. In this one, the secret is the coffee.

HOLIDAY EGGNOG

4 large eggs, separated
½ cup granulated sugar
1⅓ cups each heavy cream, milk, and
    brandy
¼ cup rum
Freshly grated nutmeg

Two hours before serving in 2-quart bowl, whisk yolks and 6 tablespoons of the sugar. Beat in cream, milk, brandy, and rum. Chill about 2 hours. Beat egg whites and remaining 2 tablespoons sugar until stiff peaks form. Gently fold into yolk mixture. Ladle into cups and sprinkle each with freshly grated nutmeg. Makes about 12 half-cup servings.

HATTIE HOFFMAN'S AMERICAN FRUITCAKE

½ pound pitted dates, halved
18 dried apricot halves, cut into thirds
10 maraschino cherries, stemmed and
    halved
½ cup dark raisins
1 teaspoon baking soda
1 cup strong, hot coffee
1½ cups all-purpose flour
1 cup chopped walnuts
¾ cup granulated sugar
2 tablespoons butter, melted and cooled
    to room temperature
1 large egg
Pinch salt

Heat oven to 325°F. (160°C). Butter and flour two 8-x-4-x 2½-inch loaf pans. In large bowl place dates, apricots, cherries, and raisins. Sprinkle with baking soda and stir in coffee.

In another bowl, stir together flour, walnuts, sugar, butter, egg, and salt. Stir into fruit mixture until well combined. Scrape into prepared pans. Smooth tops with spatula. Bake 1 hour or until toothpick inserted in center comes out clean. Makes 2 fruitcakes.

PUMPKIN BISQUE

1 1-pound can plain pumpkin
1½ cups heavy cream
1 cup chicken broth, canned or
    homemade
2 tablespoons packed brown sugar
½ teaspoon salt
½ teaspoon ground cinnamon
¼ teaspoon each ground ginger and
    nutmeg
Parsley leaves for garnish

In a 4-quart saucepan whisk all ingredients except parsley. Bring to a boil over medium heat, stirring constantly. Boil one minute. Ladle into soup bowls, garnish with parsley leaves. Makes about 4 cups.

CANADIAN MAPLE PIE

¼ cup butter, at room temperature
½ cup granulated sugar
3 large eggs
1 cup pure maple syrup
1 cup coarsely chopped pecans
1 9-inch unbaked pie shell
½ cup whipped cream

Heat oven to 400°F. (200°C). In bowl of electric mixer, cream butter and sugar; beat in remaining ingredients except whipped cream. Pour into pie shell. Bake 40 to 50 minutes or until set and crust is golden.

Cool on wire rack. Just before serving garnish with a border of whipped cream. Makes 8 servings.

TRADITIONAL TOURTIÈRE

1½ pounds ground lean pork
1 small onion, minced
1 clove garlic, chopped
¼ teaspoon ground cinnamon
Pinch ground cloves
¼ teaspoon celery salt
¼ teaspoon black pepper
¼ teaspoon sage, crumbled
1½ teaspoon salt
½ cup boiling water
3 medium potatoes, peeled and cubed
Pastry for a double crust 9-inch pie
1 large egg beaten with 1 tablespoon milk
    for egg glaze

In a heavy 5-quart saucepan or Dutch oven, combine the first 9 ingredients and cook over low heat, stirring constantly, until the meat loses its pink color. Add water, cover and cook about 45 minutes longer or until about half the liquid has been absorbed. Meanwhile, boil, drain, and mash potatoes. Stir into cooked meat mixture. Cool. Prepare pastry for a double-crust 9-inch pie. Heat oven to 450°F. (230°C). Roll out half and line a deep 9-inch pie plate or oval casserole. Fill with cooled meat mixture. Cover with remaining rolled out pastry. Flute and seal edges. Slash top crust. Decorate top with pastry leaf, if desired. Brush with egg glaze. Bake 10 minutes. Reduce heat to 350° F (180° C) and bake 30 to 40 minutes longer.

(*Tourtieres* were originally made with large birds called *tourtes* until these became extinct.)

Gaily decorated packages under the tree.

Giving

Although the custom of exchanging greeting cards originated in England, nowhere is it more popular than in the United States. Americans send greeting cards to mark many different occasions and celebrations, but the winter holiday season is the time for encompassing family, friends, business colleagues or customers, and anyone else to whom one wishes to give a joyful message.

In 1949 when Maurice Pate was Executive Director of UNICEF, he selected a cheerful piece of art by a little Czech girl, Jitka Samkova, and had it reproduced and sold as a greeting card to benefit UNICEF. Jitka had sent her art in gratitude for food received through UNICEF immediately following World War II. Thus began the custom of making and selling greeting cards to benefit special causes.

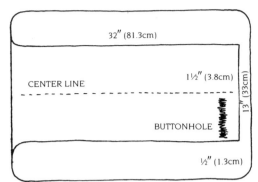

CARD TREE

To show off those most traditional of American holiday gifts—greeting cards—one can make a card tree of cloth that collapses and stores easily. It can also be washed at the beginning of each holiday season.

Materials: 2¼ yds. (2.06m) green cotton, muslin, synthetic, or blend [ideal width is 42″ (106.7cm) but pattern can be adjusted for fabric widths from 36″ to 45″ (91.5 to 114.3cm)]; 1 sheet Foam Core 36″ by 24″ (91.5 by 60.9cm)—available from art supply shops—or lightweight particle board or thin plywood; 1 wooden dowel, ⅛″ (.3cm) diameter by 6″ (15.2cm) long; green thread—1 spool; green or red yarn for hanging tree; darning needle.

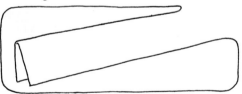

1. Cut fabric into 3 equal widths of 14″ (35.5cm).
2. Fold one piece in half lengthwise, right sides together. Cut length to 73″ (185.5cm), making sure top and bottom edges are perfectly straight. This piece will be outer frame of tree.

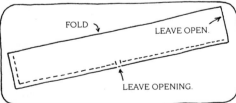

3. Sew seams along two edges as shown; interrupt seam at middle of long side and leave ½″ (1.3cm) opening. Make seams no wider than ½″ (1.3cm).

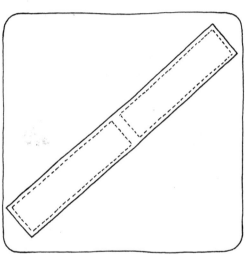

4. Trim corners. Turn right side out. Press carefully so all corners and edges are smooth and even. Be especially sure the bottom edges are neatly pressed inside before sewing bottom rectangle (Step 5).
5. Stitch neatly around top and bottom rectangles as shown. Width between side seams should be 6″ (15.2cm). Finished length should be 72″ (183cm).

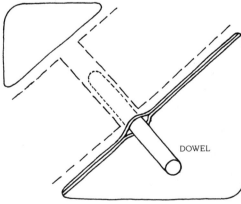

6. Test to be sure dowel fits inside opening at middle.

7. From remaining two 14″ x 81″ (35.5 x 206cm) fabric strips, cut 6 pieces each 13″ (33cm) high and 32″, 27″, 22″, 17″, 12″, and 7″ (81.3, 68.6, 55.9, 43.2, 30.5, and 17.8cm) wide. With right side of fabric up, machine sew a buttonhole in lower right corner of each piece. Start ½″ (1.3cm) from bottom and 1½″ (3.8cm) from right side; end exactly at center line, as indicated in diagram, for 32″ (81.3cm) piece. The buttonhole will be approximately 6″ (15.2cm) long.
8. Slit each buttonhole open.

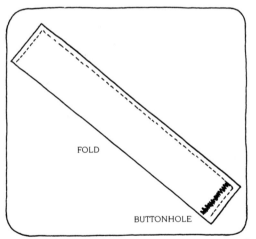

9. Fold each piece up along center line and baste or pin in place. Wrong side of fabric is now up.
10. Sew ½″ (1.3cm) seam along top and both sides. Buttonholes should extend from fold to seam, but not beyond.
11. Trim corners and turn right side out. Press well, making sure corners are square and sides straight.
12. To make shelves, cut Foam Core, particle board, or thin plywood into 6 pieces, each 6″ (15.2cm) wide and 30″, 25″, 20″, 15″, 10″, and 5″ (76.2, 63.5, 50.8, 38.1, 25.4, and 12.7cm) long.

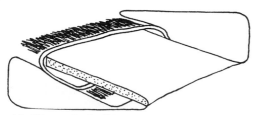

13. Slip each shelf into its appropriate fabric sleeve, through the buttonholes. Gently ease the 2 corners just beyond the buttonhole over the board corners. The fit should be snug and tight, with the seams lining up with the edges of the boards.

14. Insert dowel into space left open in middle of 72" (183cm) frame piece. Using a darning needle, thread yarn into fabric under dowel, at middle point of dowel. Tie directly over dowel and then tie again higher up on yarn, making a loop for hanging. Length will depend on how high or low you wish tree to hang.

15. Starting from bottom, baste into place the 6 shelves at 6" (15.2cm) intervals on the inside sides of the frame. Before basting, check to make sure that all seams are toward back of tree, and that buttonholes are on under side of shelves. It will take some adjusting and re-basting before shelves line up straight.

16. When you are quite sure shelves are carefully aligned, stitch at each shelf end. (You may wish to take out boards to make stitching easier.) Stitch neatly through both thicknesses of frame.

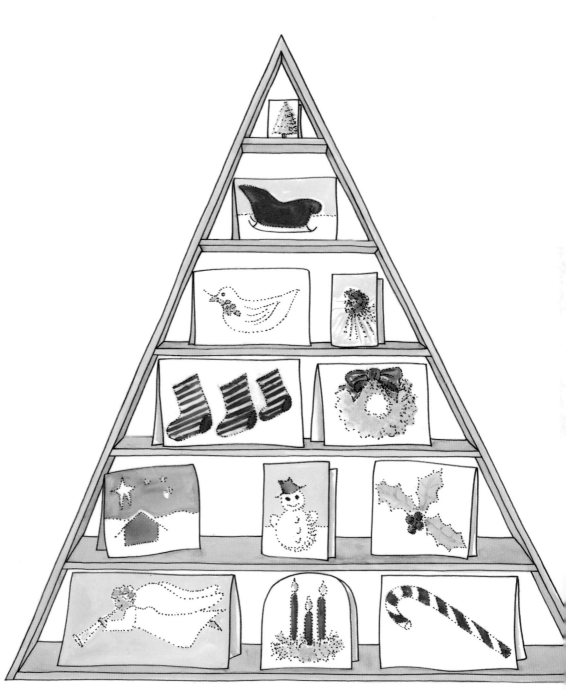

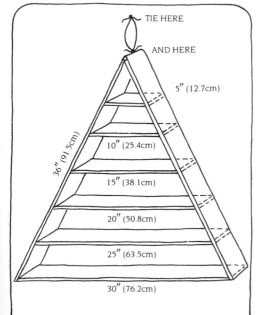

In the days before Christmas many families in the U.S. and Canada exchange colorful cards some of which are purchased from UNICEF to help support children in need throughout the world. This card tree of green fabric offers a way to display cards received during the holidays.

Hang card tree and display cards on shelves or pin along sides.

Christmas West

As earlier chapters have related, the celebrations surrounding Christmas extend to every corner of the globe and incorporate many features of ancient folklore and legend. We can cover only some of the best known traditional Christmas celebrations in *Joy Through the World*, but virtually every country and every people that have come under the influence of Christianity developed unique customs, festive foods, and festive gifts and decorations which the venturesome reader may want to explore further. Here, for a teaser, are some glimpses of Christmas as celebrated in a few other countries of the world. We also include in this chapter a relatively new holiday, begun in the United States in the 1960s and celebrated on the day after Christmas. Called Kwanzaa, it is a nonreligious celebration of the home, the family, and the African cultural heritage of black Americans.

Celebrations, Feasting, and Giving

France

In France Pere Noël (Father Christmas) along with his assistant Père Fouettard (loosely translated as "Father Whip") keep track of children's behavior during the year and bestow gifts on good boys and girls. The pair visit households on December 6th, St. Nicholas Eve, leaving small gifts in children's shoes. In some families children have a second chance to be rewarded on Christmas Eve, when *le petit Jésus* leaves tokens.

Christmas Eve centers around Midnight Mass, followed by a late supper called the *Réveillon*, or "Wake-up." Roast goose almost always graces the table, because, according to ancient lore, a gaggle of geese welcomed the Wise Men as they approached the stable where Jesus was born. The rest of the meal may include expensive delicacies such as truffles, foie gras, and shellfish. Christmas Day is the occasion for another special, if somewhat lighter, meal at midday. But caution is thrown to the winds at the end when the cook presents the traditional *Bûche de Noël*. This dessert, sculpted in the form of a yule log, consists of a filled sponge-cake roll frosted with a barklike surface of mocha butter cream and decorated with marzipan green leaves and red cherries.

Greece

Christmas begins in earnest in this Mediterranean country on Christmas Eve, when young boys go caroling from house to house, singing the good news of Christ's birth and collecting coins for themselves. Church services and Christmas Eve dinner follow. Considering that the Greeks are coming out of a forty-day fast when they sit down to this meal, it's not surprising that each dish is accorded

Crèche (wood carving), Nigeria.

enthusiastic reception. Among the traditional dishes served are *Christopsomo*, Christmas bread, *melomacaroma*, Christmas biscuits, and *kourabiedes*, crescent-shaped cookies. The last-named are studded with cloves as a reminder of the spices brought by the Wise Men to the Baby Jesus.

The twelve days between Christmas and Epiphany are a time for being vigilant against *kallikantzare*, mischievous creatures who descend on earth at year's end to put out cooking fires, break dishes, knock over chairs, lose things, and cause other minor mishaps around the house. To ward the pests off, Greeks keep a sprig of basil wound around a wooden cross and dip it in water daily, sprinkling the magic water about. And because *kallikantzare* are repulsed by the smell of meat, some traditionalists burn an old shoe and hang pork bones in the chimney. The most important protection of all, Greeks assure us, is to keep the fire burning day and night until after Epiphany. This will keep the goblins from slipping in by way of the chimney. A tangle of flax over the door is another form of insurance. It seems that *kallikantzare* cannot resist trying to undo the tangle, and this activity keeps them busy until sunrise when they must go into hiding again.

Gifts are exchanged on January 1st, the name day of St. Basil, who is the patron saint of the poor and idigent. Dinner that day is likely to conclude with the traditional *Basilópitta*, or "Basil's Cake." Baked with a trinket or coin inside to symbolize St. Basil's generosity, it must be sliced according to ritual: the first piece set aside for St. Basil, the second for the poor, the third given to the oldest member of the household, and so on, down the line to the youngest child. Whoever gets the prize is assured good luck in the New Year. If St. Basil is the winner, then a donation must be given to the Church. A recipe for Basilópitta follows. With slight modification, the same cake is known in Germany as *Dreikönigsbrot*, and in Mexico as *Rosca de Reyes* (both of which translate as Three Kings' Bread). It is served on January 6th, Epiphany, which in Greece is also the day on which the Church commemorates Christ's baptism. The Greek Epiphany brings to an official close the Christmas season.

Outdoor crèche, Barcelona, Spain.

Holiday service at the Church of the Holy Saviour, Ethiopia.

Philippines

Filipinos like to say that they devote more days of the year to Christmas than do any other people. Whatever the truth of the assertion, there's no doubt that the season here is a long one. Christmas observances begin on December 16th with church bells heralding the first of nine masses leading up to Christmas Eve. Held very early in the morning, "at the cock's crow," these services are well-attended, in fact so well that a small industry of street vendors burgeons every December around each church. They sell roasted and baked rice cakes and ginger tea to the hungry Christians emerging from Mass.

Decorations, especially many-colored lights, are hung lavishly around doorways, in windows, on lamp posts, and over the fronts of stores and public buildings. Almost every house has its own *belen*, or crèche, either outside in the yard or inside in a place of honor. Star lanterns, some small and made of bamboo frames with a candle inside, some extremely large and lighted with electric bulbs, are the obvious favorite ornaments everywhere. In at least one community, San Fernando, Pampanga, near Manila, the making of lanterns has evolved into a joyful extravaganza. Groups of people combine to construct lanterns "as big as houses," and on Christmas Eve the lanterns are mounted on trucks and driven through town to the accompaniment of dancers, singers, and celebrants.

Christmas Eve concludes with Mass and an elaborate meal. Christmas Day is a time for children to pay their respects to their godparents and for adults to hold open houses for one another. The season ends with Three Kings Day, January 6th, when richly-costumed Magi ride through the streets distributing gifts to the children and alms to the poor.

Child admiring Christmas wares. Strasbourg, France.

Portuguese crèche.

PHILIPPINE CHRISTMAS STAR

Materials: ten 36" x ¼" (91 x .5cm) dowels; five 5" x ¼" (13 x .5cm) dowels; two 3' (91cm)-wide rolls of plain gift wrap or cellophane in contrasting colors; roll of white crepe or tissue; eight 4" x 24" (10 x 61cm) strips of green crepe; scissors; picture wire; household glue; 2 thin-wire coathangers; forty ½" x 36" (1 x 91cm) strips of cellophane or foil.

Note: the authentic Philippine star is of these dimensions, but you can reduce the size if you wish.

Making the Christmas star

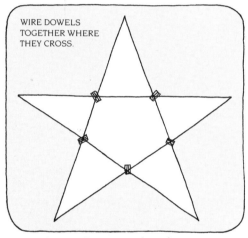

WIRE DOWELS TOGETHER WHERE THEY CROSS.

1. Lay five 36" (91cm) dowels across one another to form a 5-point star. At each of 5 places where dowels cross, tie them together with wire. Make an identical star with other 5 dowels.

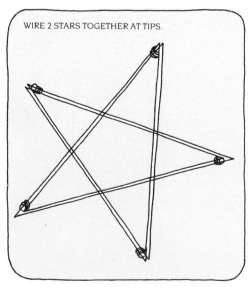

WIRE 2 STARS TOGETHER AT TIPS.

2. Place 1 star on top of the other and wire 4 dowels of the 5 points together.

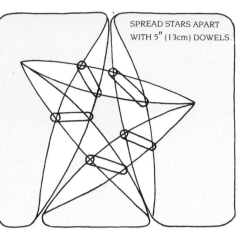

SPREAD STARS APART WITH 5" (13cm) DOWELS.

3. Use 5" (13cm) dowels to spread centers of stars apart. Apply glue to both ends and put in place between top and bottom star where 36" (91cm) dowels cross.

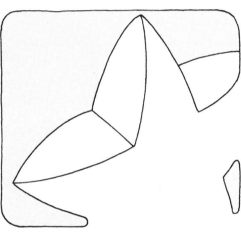

4. Cut 3' (91cm) square piece of gift wrap or cellophane. Apply glue along dowels on front of star and glue paper or cellophane in place. When dry, trim off excess gift wrap. Turn star over and repeat on back using different color.

5. From white crepe or tissue, cut 10 triangles approximately 15" x 5" (38 x 18cm). Glue 1 piece on each side of point between top and bottom stars. Trim off edges. Repeat for 4 other points.

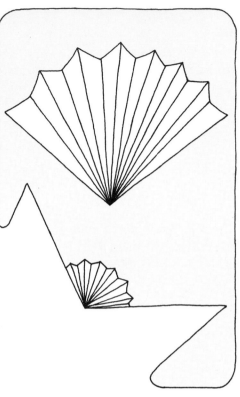

6. To decorate, from white or colored paper cut 5 rectangles 5" (13cm) high with 10" (25cm) bases. Fold each into tight fan shape and glue between adjacent arms of star. Cut symmetrical or floral designs and glue to both faces of star.

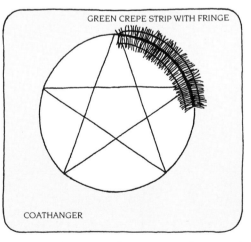

GREEN CREPE STRIP WITH FRINGE

COATHANGER

7. Straighten coathangers and curve 1 around half of star wiring it to tips with picture wire. Twist together with end of second coathanger and proceed around star. With scissors, make fringe on long sides of green crepe strips and glue to front of coathangers. Repeat for back.

136

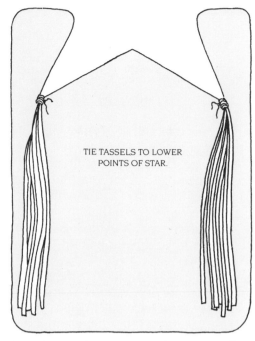

TIE TASSELS TO LOWER
POINTS OF STAR.

8. To form 18" (46cm) tassels, tie 20 cellophane or foil strips together at center and tie to one of star's lower points. Repeat for other lower point.

9. Attach loop of picture wire to top point and hang star on wall or from ceiling.

Note: the authentic Philippine star is of these dimensions, but you can reduce the size if you wish.

The farol (star) originated in Spain with an early Renaissance custom of Christmas celebration. Groups of minstrels carrying stars performed at the courts of the Spanish nobility. When Spain colonized the Philippean islands after they were discovered by Magellen in 1521, the old custom was adapted on a grand scale by the people of the new land.

Kwanzaa

Beginning on December 26th, many black Americans celebrate Kwanzaa, a holiday that originated in the United States at the height of the civil rights movement in the 1960s and commemorates their African heritage. Created out of rituals borrowed from African harvest festivals, and using the language of Swahili to designate its symbols and customs, Kwanzaa continues for a week, during which participants gather with family and friends to exchange gifts and to light a series of black, red, and green candles symbolizing the seven basic values of black American family life—unity, self-determination, collective work and responsibility, cooperative economics, purpose, creativity, and faith.

In the days just before the start of Kwanzaa, the whole family joins in decorating the house with all manner of black, red, and green paper decorations. Some families also hang homemade ornaments on an evergreen "Kwanzaa bush." A principal point of the holiday is to educate children about their heritage, and many households seize the day to display African artwork and in other ways pay tribute to Africa, past and present. They also set out photographs of recent generations of the family. The mother of the family sets a ceremonial table, placing on it an ear of corn to symbolize each of her children, and a carved and decorated unity cup, or *kikombe*, with which toasts will be made each evening.

Then, on seven consecutive nights beginning with December 26th, the family gathers to light the *kinara*, or seven-holed candleholder. On the first night one of the children is asked to light the central—black—candle, symbolizing unity, after which the parents talk about the meaning of the word. On the next night someone lights a red one, to represent self-determination, and so on through the seven nights. Each night the parents lead the family in talking about what the evening's central idea means to each person in the room.

And each night, everyone also drinks from the unity cup which is filled with a *tambico*, or libation; as it passes around the table, parents reminisce about members of the family, saluting especially those whose lives may be in some way inspirational.

December 31st is the night for the giving of *zawadi*, or gifts, mostly to the children. The gifts traditionally include a book and a heritage symbol, such as an African art object, and something homemade. A Kwanzaa slogan, "You must achieve to receive," is taken very seriously in some families, who reward their children in direct proportion to their accomplishments. Other households, particularly those that do not also celebrate Christmas, exercise much more latitude in giving to youngsters, and the usual sorts of toys, games, and dolls are likely to turn up amongst the *zawadi*. The seven-day celebration ends later in the evening with a feast. It's a happy time with many friends and family gathered together, a table set lavishly with African and black American foods, and plenty of music—usually a mix of black American and African sounds. When everyone has finished eating, they rise together, recommit themselves to the seven principles of Kwanzaa, and bid each other happy months ahead. The host ends the formal part of the party with the wish that "at the end of this year, may we sit again together, in larger numbers, with greater achievement ... and a higher level of human life."

KWANZAA: MAKING
THE KINARA (candleholder)

Materials: self-hardening clay; pointed clay modeling tool or orange stick; tempera or acrylic paints in several colors (red, black, and green are the traditional Kwanzaa colors); paint brushes; 7 candles.

Making the kinara

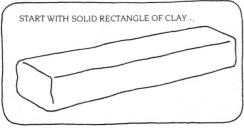

START WITH SOLID RECTANGLE OF CLAY...

1. Spread newspapers over work area.
2. Following instructions that come with clay, form a base for kinara by shaping a solid rectangle. A good size is 12" (30cm) long, 2" (5cm) high, and 2" (5cm) thick, but you can choose your own dimensions.

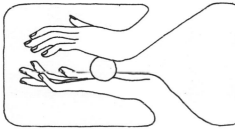

3. To make holders for the 7 candles, roll 7 clay balls each about 1" (2½cm) in diameter.

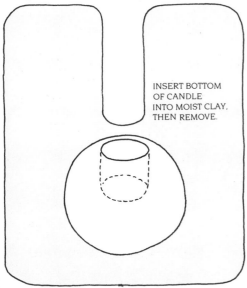

INSERT BOTTOM OF CANDLE INTO MOIST CLAY, THEN REMOVE.

4. Before the balls harden, insert the end of a candle into each ball and then remove it.

MOISTEN BOTTOMS OF CANDLEHOLDERS AND STICK THEM ON RECTANGLE.

5. Glue candleholders to base using water, which will make the pieces stick together.

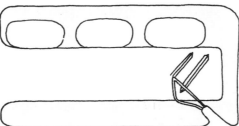

6. While clay is still wet, decorate base with incised designs using clay modeling tool.

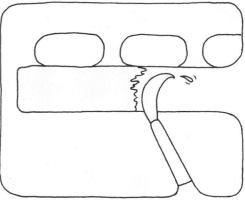

7. After clay hardens, paint base and candleholders. When paint is dry, insert candles.

Traditionally, the kinara is placed on a straw mat symbolizing tradition. It is surrounded by an ear of corn for each child in the family; a unity cup, the kikombe, made of wood or coconut; and tropical fruits and vegetables.

Kwanzaa is a new tradition celebrated in the last week of December. It draws its symbols from black cultures, including gifts made—not bought—and, as shown here, a row of candles to be lighted on each of the seven days after Christmas.

139

On the kitchen marble are (clockwise from lower left) Greek kourabiedes, almond-flavored shortbread ovals; a French Buche de Noel, the traditional Yule Log; and a lime-flavored Philippine flan (caramel custard). Sprinkle powdered sugar on the shortbread and Buche de Noel. The flan is garnished with thin slivers of lime peel.

FRENCH BÛCHE DE NOËL

Cake

3 large eggs
6 tablespoons granulated sugar
¾ cup all-purpose flour
1 teaspoon baking powder
¼ cup raspberry jam

Icing

½ cup unsalted butter, at room
　temperature
2 cups powdered sugar
1 tablespoon unsweetened cocoa powder
　or 1 tablespoon instant coffee granules
　dissolved in 1 tablespoon water
Meringue Mushrooms (optional garnish,
　recipe below)

Heat oven to 400°F. (200°C). Grease a jelly-roll pan, line with waxed paper, and grease that. With electric mixer, beat eggs until tripled in volume. Beat in sugar gradually until mixture becomes thick. Mix flour and baking powder; gently fold into egg mixture with rubber spatula. Scrape into prepared pan and smooth evenly with metal spatula. Bake 7 minutes or until lightly browned and cake tests done. Invert cake onto waxed paper sprinkled lightly with sugar. Trim ends off cake. Spread jam evenly on cake and roll up from long end. Let cool. Meanwhile, prepare icing. Cream butter with electric mixer; gradually add sugar and cocoa powder or dissolved coffee until smooth. Spread onto cooled cake. Make lines on icing with fork to simulate bark. Dust with additional powdered sugar and decorate with Meringue Mushrooms, if desired. Makes 10 servings.

FRENCH MERINGUE MUSHROOMS

Whites of 4 large eggs
1 cup granulated sugar
Few drops lemon juice
Unsweetened cocoa powder

Heat oven to 200°F (93°C). Butter and flour a cookie sheet. Set aside. Beat egg whites and lemon juice with electric mixer until foamy. Gradually beat in sugar until mixture forms stiff and shiny peaks. Fit a pastry bag with a small plain tube and fill the tube with meringue. Pipe small rounds for "caps" and short tubes for "stems." Bake about 1 hour until dry on the outside and still soft inside. Cool slightly. Attach stems to caps by pressing them gently together. Sift cocoa powder over tops to color, if desired. Use mushrooms to decorate Bûche de Noël if desired.

MTEDZA MALAWI (GROUND NUT CHICKEN)

A 2½-to-3 pound chicken, cut in 8 pieces
¼ cup all-purpose flour
½ teaspoon salt
¼ teaspoon freshly ground pepper
3 tablespoons vegetable oil
2 cups finely chopped peanuts
1 can (13 to 14 ounces) chicken broth or
　1¾ cups homemade
1 large onion, chopped
4 tomatoes, chopped
1 small hot red chili pepper, seeded and
　chopped
3 sliced hard-cooked eggs
1 orange, sliced
Hot cooked rice
Nsima

Heat oven to 350°F. (180°C). Dredge chicken lightly in flour seasoned with salt and pepper. Heat ¼-inch oil in large, heavy skillet over high heat. Add chicken and cook on all sides until brown. Transfer chicken to a 3-quart casserole. In medium bowl, mix peanuts with broth, onion, tomatoes, and chopped chili. Pour over chicken. Cover and bake about 1 hour or until chicken is tender. Garnish with sliced egg and oranges. Serve with cooked rice and Nsima. Makes 6 servings.

NSIMA (THICK CORNMEAL PORRIDGE)

9 cups water
3 cups yellow cornmeal
1 tablespoon peanut oil

Heat water in 6-quart saucepot until simmering. Slowly stir in cornmeal in a slow, steady stream, so there are no lumps. Cook over low heat, stirring, until thick and smooth and cornmeal has no gritty taste. Stir in peanut oil. Serve alongside Ground Nut Chicken.

PHILIPPINE FLAN (CARAMEL CUSTARD)

½ cup plus 3 tablespoons granulated
　sugar
1 pint heavy cream
yolks of 6 large eggs
1 tablespoon fresh-squeezed lime juice
½ teaspoon grated lime peel
Thin strands lime peel, optional garnish

Heat oven to 350°F. (180°C). Make a caramel, rich golden brown in color, using ½ cup sugar dissolved in about 3 tablespoons water. Pour into 1-quart baking dish; swirl the dish to coat bottom and sides evenly; set aside. Scald cream. Beat yolks and remaining 3 tablespoons sugar; slowly beat in scalded cream. Stir in juice and grated lime peel. Pour mixture into prepared baking dish. Set dish into a shallow pan of hot water. Bake about 1 hour or until nearly set in center. Flan will continue to cook out of oven. Cool slightly. Chill. Garnish with lime peel, if desired. Serves 6.

GREEK KOURABIEDES

½ cup sweet butter
¼ cup powdered sugar
½ teaspoon vanilla extract
¼ teaspoon almond extract
1 cup all-purpose flour
¼ teaspoon baking powder
Additional powdered sugar

In bowl of electric mixer, cream butter and powdered sugar until light and fluffy. Beat in vanilla and almond extracts. Stir flour and baking powder and gently fold into sugar mixture. Chill 30 minutes. Heat oven to 325°F. (160°C). Form into 1-inch ovals. Place 2 inches apart on ungreased baking sheet. Bake 20 to 25 minutes until lightly golden. Cool on rack. Dust with powdered sugar, if desired. Makes about 20 cookies.

Anonymous embroidery, nineteenth century, Greece.

Anonymous ceramic tile, Museo Nacional de Artes Decorativas (Madrid), Spain.

North African crèche.

143

Grandfather Frost

New Year's Day has largely replaced Christmas as the major winter festival in the Soviet Union. The day is especially important to children, for it is on the first day of the New Year that Grandfather Frost visits, bringing gifts. Adding to youngsters' pleasure, schools close down for a long vacation in late December, signaling the start of government-sponsored parties and special children's theatricals and other entertainments in towns and cities all over this vast country.

Celebration

Of all the official New Year's celebrations in the USSR, none is staged with greater panache and style than the party given within the walls of Moscow's Kremlin in the modern Palace of Congresses. As many as 50,000 attendance tickets are sold in the weeks before the annual event, and parents go to great lengths to snap them up before they're gone.

For the occasion, the huge hall is transformed into a fairyland. A towering New Year's Tree, as high as 75 feet, stands in the center of the hall. As on Christmas trees of European tradition, garlands of glittering balls, tinsel, and colored lights festoon its spreading branches.

As each child presents a ticket to the clown at the door, he or she is handed a gaily wrapped gift. Then everyone jostles for a place to stand and watch the entertainment. First comes D'yed Moroz, or Grandfather Frost, with white beard and a brilliant red robe and hat rimmed in white fur. His arrival, aboard a Sputnik-drawn sleigh or some other fantastical conveyance, is staged with great fanfare. He is followed by a dozen or more attendants, including the Snow Maiden, snow bunnies, and a clown, and costumed youngsters—boys in old time peasant tunics, baggy pants, and boots, girls in pinafores and blouses.

Moscow New Year's Tree No. 1. A scene of the New Year's Festival in the Kremlin Palace of Congresses.

Then on the stage at one end of the hall troops of folk dancers glide into sight, their feet flying across the floor to the sound of *balalaikas* and *gusli*. Choruses from far-off provinces present their wonderful melodies; magicians, clowns, and tumblers all perform, to the great delight of the children and their parents.

The Kremlin party is geared mostly to younger Muscovites. Older children and young adults have dances to go to—at schools, clubs, theaters, and union halls. Intermissions feature wonderful food and a variety of entertainments, and everyone stays up very late. Far beyond Moscow, at farm collectives, at factories, and in mining communities, the story is much the same but on a more modest scale, as young and old alike gather to mark the start of the New Year. Everywhere, holiday decorations—lights, paper lanterns, evergreen boughs, and New Year's trees—brighten public buildings.

Quite apart from the public celebrations, stores selling toys, games, books, and candy are decorated for the season, and they do the briskest trade of the year in the few days just preceding the festivities.

Father Frost and the Snow Maiden, laquered box cover by Mrs. Yerova from Palekh (USSR).

Schoolchildren during the New Year's celebration in the Column Hall of the Palace of Unions, Moscow.

146

Feasting

Caviar, smoked fish, roast meats, and other treats are served in honor of the holiday. Fresh fruits, rare in this country in winter and consequently rather expensive, make welcome gifts; they may also be offered at home to special friends and relatives. Among the many cakes and sweets served at this season are *babka* and *kulich*. *Babka* is a raised coffee cake made in a deep round pan. The name derives from the Russian word for grandmother and refers, one supposes, to the plump, wide-skirted, grandmotherly shape of the finished cake. *Kulich* is a fancy, fruited bread of Ukrainian origin once closely associated with Christian Christmas and Easter but now a treat for all seasons. *Kulich* is traditionally made in three tiers, the three an emblem of the Trinity, the circle symbolizing eternity. Sometimes three separate rings of braided bread are used to create the holiday treat, but a simpler, quite acceptable method is to bake a single, rather high, cake and slice it crosswise to make the three layers. A candle traditionally tops the cake when it is presented at table.

This feast is extravagant, but if snow piles up outside your window, what is more comforting than (top center) a bowl of hot borsch, *a stack of feather-light* bliny *garnished with sour cream and caviar, beef- and pork-filled miniature dumplings* (pal'meni), *yeasty Russian* pierozhki *(upper left) filled with cabbage and egg, and a delicately garnished platter of jellied sturgeon? A shot of vodka and . . .
Na starovya!!*

BLINY

2¾ cups milk
1 package active dry yeast
4 cups all-purpose flour
2 large eggs, separated
1½ tablespoons butter, melted
1 tablespoon granulated sugar
¾ teaspoon salt
Vegetable oil
Caviar
Sour cream
Melted butter

Heat 1 cup milk to 105 to 115°F. (41 to 46°C). Pour into a large bowl. Stir in yeast and 2 cups flour until smooth. Cover bowl and put in warm place for about 1 hour until batter has doubled in size. Stir down with wooden spoon; stir in yolks, butter, sugar, salt, and remaining flour alternating with remaining 1¾ cups milk until nearly smooth. Cover bowl and put in warm place 45 minutes to 1 hour until doubled in size. Stir down batter. Beat egg whites until stiff; fold into batter.

On lightly greased griddle or skillet over medium heat fry batter, using about ⅓ cup for each bliny. Fry about 4 minutes, turning once, until browned and spotted. Keep bliny warm in low oven while continuing with remaining batter. Serve in a stack. Garnish with caviar and/or sour cream and/or melted butter. Makes twenty four 5-inch pancakes.

PEL'MENI

About ½ pound ground beef (or ¼ pound
    each ground beef and pork)
1 small onion, chopped
½ teaspoon salt
⅛ teaspoon fresh ground black pepper
1½ cups all-purpose flour
1 large egg
3 tablespoons cold water
Sour cream

In lightly greased 6-inch skillet sauté ground beef and onion about 10 minutes until no longer pink and meat is cooked through. Season with salt and pepper. In container of food processor, process ground mixture until nearly smooth, or mince very finely with a chef's knife. Set aside. In medium bowl, make a dough with flour, egg, and water. Knead (on lightly floured surface, if necessary) until smooth and elastic. Let rest, lightly covered, about 15 minutes. Cut dough in half. Roll one piece less than ⅛-inch thick and cut out about 24 to 36 two-inch rounds. Put about ½ teaspoon meat filling in center of each round; fold over and pinch edges together tightly. Repeat with remaining dough and filling. (These may be wrapped and frozen at this point.) To cook, drop into boiling salted water and simmer 8 to 10 minutes, until dough is cooked and filling is heated through. Drain and serve with sour cream, if desired. Makes about 70.

BORSCH

1 pound lean brisket of beef
1 bay leaf
3 tablespoons butter
1 cup chopped onion
1 pound beets, peeled and cubed
1 carrot, diced
1 parsnip, diced
½ cup tomato paste
¼ cup red wine vinegar
4 cups chopped cabbage
3 cups diced potatoes
2 tomatoes, peeled, seeded, and diced
½ teaspoon salt
Freshly ground pepper to taste
½ cup sour cream
¼ cup chopped fresh parsley

Put brisket and bay leaf in Dutch oven. Add water to cover and bring to a boil over high heat. Lower heat to a simmer, cover, and cook 1 to 1½ hours or until fork-tender. Meanwhile, melt butter in a heavy skillet. Add onion and sauté 5 minutes until soft. Add beets, carrot, parsnip, tomato paste, and vinegar. Stir well to combine. Cover and cook over low heat 30 to 40 minutes or until soft. Remove brisket from pot; cube and return to broth. Add cabbage, potatoes, salt, and pepper. Stir in beet mixture. Bring to a boil. Reduce heat to low, cover, and simmer 15 to 20 minutes or until cabbage and potatoes are soft. Add diced tomatoes and cook 5 minutes more. Garnish each soup bowl with a little sour cream and parsley. Makes 6 to 8 servings.

CABBAGE PIEROZHKI

1 envelope active dry yeast
1 cup warm milk
1 large egg
¼ cup butter
1½ teaspoons granulated sugar
1½ teaspoons salt
About 4¼ cups all-purpose flour
4 cups cabbage, chopped
1 small onion, chopped
¼ teaspoon freshly ground black pepper
1 hard-cooked egg, chopped
1 large egg beaten with 1 tablespoon milk

In large bowl, dissolve yeast in warm milk. Stir in egg, 2 tablespoons of the butter, sugar, and ½ teaspoon salt. Stir in flour until a dough is formed that no longer sticks to sides of bowl. Turn dough out onto a lightly floured surface and knead about 5 to 8 minutes or until smooth and elastic. Form into a ball and place in a lightly greased bowl. Turn to grease top. Cover with plastic wrap and let rise in a warm place about 1 hour or until doubled in bulk. Punch down and let rise again, covered, until doubled. Meanwhile, make cabbage filling. In large skillet, melt remaining 2 tablespoons butter. Sauté cabbage and onion 10 to 15 minutes or until cooked down to about 1½ cups, stirring occasionally. Season with 1 teaspoon salt and the pepper. Transfer to a bowl. Stir in chopped egg and let cool to room temperature. Punch down dough. Heat oven to 375°F. (190°C). Roll half the dough ¼-inch thick on lightly floured surface and cut into twenty 3½- x 2¼-inch ovals. Reroll and cut scraps if necessary. Place 10 of the ovals 1 inch apart on lightly greased baking sheets. Place 1 tablespoon cabbage filling in center of each. Brush edges with egg glaze and cover with remaining ovals. Repeat with remaining dough. Let rise about 20 minutes. Brush tops with egg glaze and bake 20 to 25 minutes or until puffed and browned. Makes 20 Pierozhki.

Grandfather Frost takes the reins.

Everyone bundles up and turns out for the New
Year's festival. Here Grandfather Frost is accompanied by a dancing bear.

Giving

One of the most beloved toys among children of the USSR is the *Matrioska* or "little mother" doll, a nesting doll that is not a single figure but a whole set of graduated-size dolls that fit one inside the next. Though the *Matrioska* must seem to most Russians to be a purely native invention of long standing, the idea is probably no more than a hundred years old and may have been inspired by the Japanese, whose beautifully made and painted nesting boxes were much prized in the West in the latter part of the nineteenth century.

The classic *Matrioska* is modeled on the lines of a plump and curvaceous grandmother. Made of thin, malleable wood, hollow on the inside, it is designed to come apart at the waist so that another doll will fit inside. On the outside it is cunningly painted with a cheery, rosy-cheeked face, a babushka covering the head, a body whose upper half is shawl and whose lower half is voluminous peasant skirt to the floor. Interior dolls, which must maintain the same lines but be progressively smaller, will sometimes have younger faces and costumes to go with them, comprising a several-generation family of dolls. Other sorts of nesting dolls are made, too, including grandfather figures, but the "little mother" version continues to be the most popular, perhaps because it recalls a character much loved in Russian folklore. A simple set of *Matrioska* consists of as many as six dolls; some of the more elaborate and skillfully made versions contain a dozen.

APPLIQUÉ AND EMBROIDERY— WALL HANGING OR PILLOW COVER

Materials: 14" (35.5cm) square of muslin, cotton, linen, or similar fabric (purchase backing fabric of same size if pillow cover is to be made); 1 small piece of plush, silk, or other fabric appropriate for the coat (approx. 5" by 8" or 12.7 by 20.3cm); embroidery thread in gold, white, off-white (or cream), black, brown, pale peach, and red (or blue) to match material selected for coat. Traditionally, the long coat of Grandfather Frost was deep blue, trimmed with white fur. It was often shown embroidered with snowflakes or stars. Of late, most Grandfather Frost depictions from the USSR show the coat in red.

1. For appliqué coat, trace outline of coat, without collar, cuffs, or hem. Make a paper pattern of tracing. Lay pattern on red (or blue) fabric and carefully cut around pattern. Center cut-out coat figure on 14" (35.5cm) square.

2. Transfer remainder of entire pattern by tracing it and then copying it onto the 14" (35.5cm) square, aligned with coat piece. Use dressmaker's carbon paper or water-soluble tracing pen. Be sure to trace snowflakes onto coat piece.

3. Appliqué coat piece using plain outline stitch in color of coat. Use outline stitch along seam lines on each side of buttons, and along fold lines at bottom of coat.

4. Embroider remaining parts of figure. Recommended colors and stitches are:

Stars and buttons—gold satin stitch
Collar, cuffs, hat, and robe edging—white long and short stitch (Kensington)
Beard, moustache, eyebrows—off-white satin stitch
Snowflakes on robe—white straight or spoke stitch
Mittens and boots—black satin stitch
Pole—brown satin stitch
Face—peach satin stitch or long and short stitch (use outline stitch for nose)
Eyes—white satin stitch
Pupils—brown satin stitch or French knot

GRANDFATHER FROST

This traditional D'yed Moroz figure has been rendered here in appliqué and embroidery. He has a white beard, fur-trimmed hat and brilliant red robe spangled with stars. This project is appropriate as a wall hanging or a pillow cover.

New Year

In Asian countries the passing of the old year and the beginning of the new is cause for the greatest celebration. Rituals, many of them evolved from beliefs that go back before recorded time, are followed in the hope of ridding oneself of the past and welcoming in the future. Everywhere the emphasis is on family, on renewing ties with distant members, and on remembering ancestors. Two countries that have particularly elaborate and interesting festivals are China and Japan.

Because the Japanese have adopted the Western calendar, their celebration is organized around January 1st. The Chinese, on the other hand, use a lunar calendar—one based on the movements of the moon—to mark traditional holidays. The first day of the month always coincides with the new moon, and New Year's, *Yuan Tan*, comes the day of the second new moon after the winter solstice, so that it falls sometime between January 21st and February 19th, the particular date changing every year. One point both cultures have in common is the Buddhist system of organizing years into twelve-year cycles, with each year coming under the special providence of an animal. The twelve creatures represented are the rat, ox, tiger, rabbit, dragon, snake, horse, ram, monkey, rooster, dog, and pig. When the year changes, so too does the spirit of the year, and the attributes associated with the new animal are believed to supersede those of the old.

Traditional Lion Dancers in Singapore.

Celebration

In prerevolutionary China, observance of the New Year began as much as a month before the actual date on the calendar. Everywhere people went through a period of energetic housecleaning, not only scrubbing down the family dwelling but also cleansing themselves in a spiritual sense by reexamining their own characters and resolving to make needed changes. By following carefully prescribed rituals, they sought to drive out evil spirits and to propitiate the benign gods in the hope that these deities would look favorably upon the family and the clan in the months to come. Just before the end of the old year, they dusted off the kitchen god, represented by a figure kept in a small niche above the hearth, and gave him a farewell dinner of sweets—that he might speak sweetly of the family in the next world. He was then set atop a bonfire in the courtyard, his smoke ascending to the heavens where, it was presumed, he would deliver his report to the rest of his godly colleagues.

Meanwhile, in the home, still other preparations were under way. Every home sported a new coat of red paint, symbol of good luck and happiness, on its front door, and scrolls of red paper hung from walls, windowsills, and door frames. Red candles, a red table cloth, and red flowers were also added to the decor. Anyone with outstanding personal debts saw to their settlement, preferably before dark on the last day. And the men, who were less busy than the women at this time, made obligatory visits to temples and distant relatives. At some point in their travels they also bought a new hearth god to put in place of the old at the appropriate moment. Because the Chinese consider New Year's Day to be everyone's birthday, the day on which everyone becomes a year older, the women of the family also had gifts to buy or make for all the others.

Finally, on the last day of the year, everyone available pitched in to complete the cooking for this day and the next—and to put away the knives for the next 24 hours, lest someone inadvertently cut good luck in the new year and bring trouble down upon the whole clan. Later, when the family was all assembled, the eldest male ceremoniously sealed the outer door with strips of red paper to keep the luck of the house in, and then the extended family settled down to a special New Year's Eve ritual consisting of prayers, offerings to ancestors, and, finally, a superb feast.

At midnight, the family rose, and the children, one by one, made formal bows to their elders. Then the eldest male broke the seal on the door—to let the good influences of the New Year in. Soon after, the streets came alive with the sounds of firecrackers. When everyone awoke the next morning, it was not only the first day of the New Year but also, in the Chinese calendar, the first day of Spring—a day thus doubly joyous.

In modern-day China, observance of New Year's Eve is less formal and time-consuming than of old, but it is still a very important and festive occasion. Firecrackers, gift giving, the hanging of pretty silk lanterns in households, and, most especially, the serving of special delicacies are as exciting today as they ever were. Temple fairs, like that held in Beijing's Ditan Park, site of the ancient Ming Dynasty Temple of the Earth, attract as many as 800,000 citizens. They come to watch bird-singing contests, fashion shows, magicians, comics, wrestlers, and jugglers and to sample the holiday specialties such as *baodu*, a delicacy made from sheep stomach, sold by hundreds of street vendors who appear for the occasion.

New Year's celebration.

A Chinese entertainer offering welcome to the New Year's dragon.

Girls in festive dress, Japan.

Female stilt-dancer with papier-maché elephant as part of her costume. She
may represent one of the Eight Immortals, characters from ancient Chinese legend.

157

Detail of New Year's parade figures.

New Year's celebration, Singapore.

The Japanese New Year, *Ganjitsu*, is also a time of renewal and excitement, but the customs surrounding it are quite different from those of the Chinese *Yuan Tan*. For example, the season begins in late November when special temple fairs liven the environment. Western Santa Clauses begin to appear, too, in stores and in advertising, giving many urban Japanese the opportunity to indulge in that very Western tradition, a Christmas shopping spree. With regard to household decorations, the Japanese hang *kumade* in early December. The *kumade* is a bamboo rake hung with lucky gods and other images; it may be only a few inches or as many as several feet in length, depending upon the owner's taste, but it must be new with each New Year. The very act of buying the *kumade* is considered portentous, too—the buyer must bargain with the seller in order to reach a price that bodes well for the buyer's prosperity in the new year.

Still other traditional decorations are purchased at the Year End Fairs. The *kadomatsu*, for example, consists of three elements: a pine branch, symbolizing long life; a bamboo stalk, emblem of prosperity, uprightness, and constancy; and an apricot or plum blossom, indicating strength and nobility. A family places two *kadomatsu* on either side of their main gate or the door of their house. Another ornament, the *shimenawa*, is a rope of rice straw. It is supposed to protect a house from harm, just as the rice-straw rope barred the cave when the ancient sun goddess, Amaterasu, threatened to go into hiding there and send the world into darkness. Plaited into its strands are strips of paper, a bitter orange, a fern frond, and a lobster, real or artificial, each element intended to insure a long and good life for every member of the family.

Along with decorating, every household traditionally goes through a *susu barai*, a ritual housecleaning, and every person does his or her best to set personal affairs

Colorful celebrant.

The art of twirling torches, Sri Lanka.

in order, too. Then on the Last Great Day all members of the family gather to eat a simple meal. As they await the midnight tolling of the temple bells, which by custom must ring 108 times to ring out the 108 worldly cares burdening human-kind, the family may visit a nearby shrine or go for a stroll. On the way home, they probably stop to have their fortunes told and perhaps to buy a tiny souvenir figure representing the new year's animal.

On New Year's morning, the male head of household draws a basin full of the first water of the year, and all family members wash their faces. Then they gather, dressed in their best clothes. After paying respect to the household shrine and to one another, they sit down to a special breakfast, including ceremonial rice wine. Afterward, they open gifts and holiday greeting cards, which are set aside until this day.

After breakfast the children have new games and toys to enjoy. Girls play a game similar to badminton, but without the net. The battledores or paddles are decorated with pictures of movie stars, beauty-contest winners, or other popular idols of the day; to the players, showing off the latest fashion in paddles seems to be at least as important as hitting the shuttlecock. Boys traditionally fly kites on New Year's Day—the more elaborate, the better. Adults visit friends and receive visitors during the day, and the hospitable table, laden with cold delicacies prepared the day before, is a matter of pride in everyone's house.

The highlight of the following day, *kakizome*, is a poem or proverb which each person composes in his or her very best calligraphic style and presents to the whole family for approval. Still more special observances follow in the next few days, with the season ending officially on January 7th when traditional decorations come down for another year.

Feasting

Few households in China today observe the ritual of banishing the old kitchen god and welcoming the new, but they still serve and enjoy special holiday foods. Spring rolls, popularly known as egg rolls in the West, are common offerings when vistors call on the first day of the New Year. Red and white dumplings, *dim sim*, filled with nuts and sugar are also favorites; their round plump shapes are seen as symbols of family cohesiveness.

The Japanese maintain some very old traditions with regard to New Year's dining. The first of these is *toshikoshi soba*, " sending out the old year noodles," which are eaten on New Year's Eve. Made of buckwheat, and longer than other kinds of noodles, they are supposed to insure good luck and long life to those who can swallow at least one strand without chewing or breaking it. Everyone also eats *mochi*, or pounded rice cakes, during the festivities. And a special two-layered rice cake, whose shape reminds the Japanese of "Amaterasu's mirror," the looking glass that supposedly enticed the sun goddess to come out of her cave and return the sun to the earth, also is a must in many households. Its origins, food historians think, are traceable to beliefs that are thousands of years old, when the winter solstice was a recurring miracle that could be explained only in tales of gods and demons.

Where East meets East, our Oriental table includes toshikoshi soba—"sending out the old year" buckwheat noodles eaten on New Year's Eve. The mochi (center foreground) are pounded rice cakes presented as a religious offering with a tangerine. On the lacquered surface are Chinese spring rolls.

A tempura meal—bits of vegetables and seafood dipped in a batter and deep-fried. The Japanese are noted for meals that are pleasing to both the palate and the eye.

LONG LIFE BUNS

3½ cups all-purpose flour
⅓ cup granulated sugar
2 tablespoons baking powder
1⅓ cups warm water
10 ounces lotus paste
Cornstarch
Red food coloring (dissolve a few drops in 1 tablespoon water)

To make dough: In medium bowl, put flour, sugar, and baking powder. Add warm water, a little at a time, stirring well to incorporate. Do not use all water if dough begins to get sticky. Knead on lightly floured surface until satiny smooth. Cut dough in half. Roll each half into a long strip and cut each into 12 pieces. Flatten pieces with fingers.
To assemble: Divide lotus paste into 24 pieces, roll each piece into a ball, and dust with cornstarch. Place balls in the center of each piece of dough. Work dough around filling, pinching edges to seal and form dumplings into a round shape. Put each finished bun on a small square of waxed or parchment paper.
To cook: Arrange buns in single layer in bamboo steamer set over rapidly boiling water. Leave space between buns; they will double in size while cooking. Steam buns 6 minutes covered. Remove from steamer and press an indentation on top of each with the back of a knife. Dot each with a little of the food-coloring mixture. Serve hot or cold. Makes 24.

SOBA NOODLES IN BROTH

1 pound soba noodles (buckwheat noodles)
4 cups Dashi or chicken broth
  ⅓ cup Japanese soy sauce
  ⅓ cup dry sherry
  2 tablespoons miso paste
  1 cup sliced scallions
  ½ cup diced tofu
  ½ teaspoon sugar

Cook noodles in boiling salted water 6 to 8 minutes or until done. Drain and rinse under warm water. Keep warm while you prepare broth. Bring remaining ingredients to a boil. Put noodles into 8 bowls; ladle hot broth over each. Makes 8 servings.

SPRING ROLLS

12 spring or egg roll wrappers
2 tablespoons peanut oil
½ cup scallions
1 cup finely shredded cabbage
1 cup bean sprouts
1 cup grated carrot
¼ cup diced bamboo shoots
2 tablespoons soy sauce
½ teaspoon salt
1 large egg
Vegetable oil for frying

Heat peanut oil in a large, heavy skillet. Add scallions and sauté until limp, 1 minute. Add cabbage, bean sprouts, carrots, and bamboo shoots. Cook until wilted. Season with soy sauce and salt. Let cool 10 minutes. Stir in egg. Place filling down center of each wrapper. Wet edges with water. Fold edges in ½-inch on sides. Roll up and seal with water, if necessary. Heat vegetable oil to 375°F. (190°C) in a large, deep skillet over high heat. Add rolls, a few at a time, and fry until golden brown. Drain on paper towels. Serve with hot mustard and duck or plum sauce. Makes 12.

JAPANESE DASHI

6 cups water
1 piece (4-inch square) dried kelp (*kombu*), washed
¾ cup shaved dried bonito (*katsuobushi*)

Put water in medium pot; add kelp and bring to boil. Remove kelp. Add bonito. Remove from heat. When bonito settles to bottom of pan, strain and use as a base for Soba Noodles in Broth (recipe). Makes 6 cups.

Long Bow Village craftsman at work spinning.The child
behind him holds a toy cat fashioned from clay.

Male stilt-dancer parading in the garb of a king.

Chengdu Lantern Festival, celebrating the Year of the Ox.

Giving

New Year's gift giving in China is on a modest scale and is mostly directed at children, who are given "red packets," attractively packaged folders containing lucky coins. Packets may turn up under pillows on New Year's morning or be handed out by visiting friends and relatives during the day.

A favorite New Year's gift for children and adults in Japan is the *daruma*. These whimsical, chubby, round-bottomed and weighted dolls are regarded as good luck charms, probably because no matter how often they are knocked over they right themselves, as though governed by some indomitable spirit. The daruma is named after Dharma, a sixth-century Indian Buddhist who is credited with founding the cult of Zen Buddhism. Legend has it that Dharma sat cross-legged in meditation for nine years as he sought serenity and balance in his life, and when he finally came out of his trance, his legs and arms were paralyzed. His only means of locomotion thereafter was rolling.

The greatest variety of darumas is to be found at New Year's fairs, but many Japanese invent and handcraft their own to give as gifts. One popular sort comes as a pair, one figure slightly larger than the other, given as a symbol of a happy marriage or happy family. Another type of daruma has an animal face painted on it; these are favorites among farmers, who keep them in the fields as scarecrows. Other darumas are demonic with fierce faces to keep away evil spirits, and still others take the form of elaborately decorated dolls with glass eyes and real hair on top. Another sort, particularly liked by children, comes with no eyes at all. The child must make a wish for the new year and then, to help the wish come true, paint one eye on the daruma. If the wish is answered, the child rewards the daruma with a second eye.

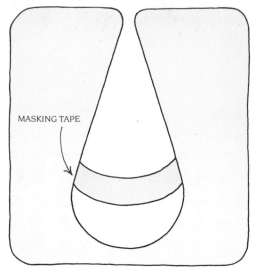

MASKING TAPE

4. After clay in bases has hardened, tape cone heads to bases.

5. Paint doll bases if you wish, and when dry, paint in mouth, eyebrows, and whiskers on coneheads. But to be authentic, do not paint in the eyes. Traditionally, one eye is painted in when the child makes a wish for the new year. The other eye is not added until the wish is fulfilled.

JAPANESE DARUMA DOLLS

Materials: one 2″ (5cm) rubber ball; utility knife; modeling clay; colored construction paper or heavy foil gift wrapping paper; scissors; household glue; masking or plastic tape; blue and red acrylic paints. Makes a pair of dolls.

Making daruma dolls

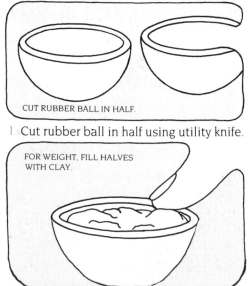

CUT RUBBER BALL IN HALF.

1. Cut rubber ball in half using utility knife.

FOR WEIGHT, FILL HALVES WITH CLAY.

2. To make doll bases, fill each ball half with modeling clay.

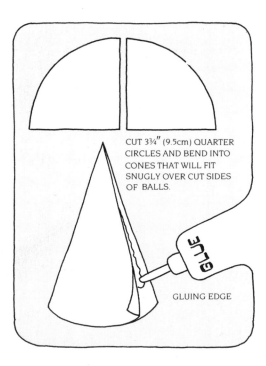

CUT 3¾″ (9.5cm) QUARTER CIRCLES AND BEND INTO CONES THAT WILL FIT SNUGLY OVER CUT SIDES OF BALLS.

GLUE

GLUING EDGE

3. To make doll heads, cut out two 3¾″ (9.5cm) quarter circles of paper with scissors, following pattern. Form into cones and glue edges of each cone together.

The daruma doll never falls down. A rubber ball on the bottom and a paper cone on the top produce a Japanese toy that will hang from a bough and entertain a child (or a cat).

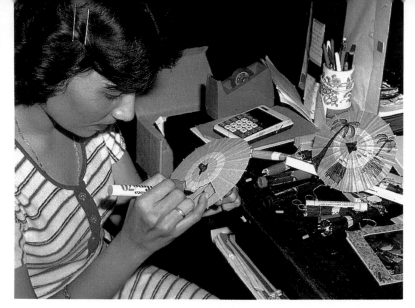

Arts and crafts for Chinese New Year.

This elaborately decorated downtown street is filled with holiday shoppers.

Here a master craftsman is working on some of the masks for which Japan is so well known.

INDEX